RHAPSODY IN BLACK

I0895552

CHINESE LITERATURE TODAY BOOK SERIES

CHINESE LITERATURE TODAY BOOK SERIES

Series Editor

Jonathan Stalling

Advisory Board

Paul B. Bell Jr., University of Oklahoma

Cao Shunqing, Sichuan University

Chen Xiaoming, Beijing University

Cheng Guangwei, Renmin University

Robert Con Davis-Undiano, *World Literature Today*

Ge Fei, Qinghua University

Peter Gries, University of Oklahoma

Howard Goldblatt, University of Notre Dame

Huang Yibing, Connecticut College

Huang Yunte, University of California, Santa Barbara

Haiyan Lee, Stanford University

Li Jingze, *People's Literature Magazine*

Liu Hongtao, Beijing Normal University

Christopher Lupke, Washington State University

Meng Fanhua, Shenyang Normal University

Haun Saussy, Yale University

Ronald Schleifer, University of Oklahoma

Daniel Simon, *World Literature Today*

Michelle Yeh, University of California, Davis

Wai-lim Yip, University of California, San Diego

Zhang Jian, Beijing Normal University

Zhang Ning, Beijing Normal University

Zhang Qinghua, Beijing Normal University

RHAPSODY IN BLACK

POEMS

By Jidi Majia

Translated by Denis Mair

Foreword by Simon J. Ortiz

UNIVERSITY OF OKLAHOMA PRESS : NORMAN

This book is published with the generous assistance of China's National Office for Teaching Chinese as a Foreign Language, Beijing Normal University's College of Chinese Language and Literature, the University of Oklahoma's College of Arts and Sciences, and *World Literature Today* magazine.

Library of Congress Cataloging-in-Publication Data

Majia, Jidi, 1961–
[Poems. Selections. English]
Rhapsody in black : poems / By Jidi Majia ; Translated by Denis Mair ;
Foreword by Simon J. Ortiz.
pages cm. — (Chinese literature today book series ; v. 3)
ISBN 978-0-8061-4449-8 (pbk. : alk. paper)
I. Mair, Denis C., translator. II. Title.
PL2948.5.J53A2 2014
895.1'16—dc23

2013035022

Rhapsody in Black: Poems is Volume 3 in the Chinese Literature Today Book Series.

The paper in this book meets the guidelines for permanence and durability of the Committee on Production Guidelines for Book Longevity of the Council on Library Resources, Inc. ∞

Copyright © 2014 by Jidi Majia. Foreword copyright © 2014 by Simon J. Ortiz; all foreword rights reserved by Simon J. Ortiz. Published by the University of Oklahoma Press, Norman, Publishing Division of the University. Manufactured in the U.S.A.

All rights reserved. No part of this publication may be reproduced, stored in a retrieval system, or transmitted, in any form or by any means, electronic, mechanical, photocopying, recording, or otherwise—except as permitted under Section 107 or 108 of the United States Copyright Act—without the prior written permission of the University of Oklahoma Press.

1 2 3 4 5 6 7 8 9 10

CONTENTS

FOREWORD

I was recently in my homeland in the southwestern region of the United States of America, where the plateau landscape is a vivid mix of mountains, valleys, canyons, and high-low desert flatlands. That is where my Indigenous community of *Aacqu* is located, along with other Indigenous Pueblo communities that are bound together by a common cultural world view. With my sisters and brothers and many relatives, that is where I was raised from infancy to adulthood. We are all part of a cultural way of life that we call the *Aacqumeh* way.

It is a cultural and terrestrial landscape storied by an ancient narrative: *uubeh-taa-neeh,* we say. Stories and more stories. The stories are everything about who we are as an *Aacqumeh hanoh.* This is who we are as an Acoma people with our own homeland. Our stories constitute what is known in American English as an oral tradition.

That is what came instantly to my mind when I read *Rhapsody in Black.* The poems in this wondrous book make me think very closely about Jidi Majia, the Nuosu poet who composed them, and whom I met at last year's Qinghai Lake International Poetry Festival. His Nuosu homelands are in the mountainous southwest region of China—but it is not only the similar landscape terrain that his poems evoke; it is also that same kind of oral tradition, the stories that are part of the cultural and terrestrial landscape so essential to the language of the poems. "Yes, like the *uubeh-taa-neeh of the Aacqumeh,*" I say to myself.

Haatse is our *Aacqumeh* word for our land. Our homeland. And when I read these lines from Majia's "A Nuosu Speaks of Fire":

> Give us blood, give us land
> O power stretching beyond antiquity
> Give us revelation, give us solace

I think to myself, this is a passionate voice that speaks for and about the *haatse.* That is the source of our voice. In fact, in a crucial sense, that voice—Jidi Majia's, and mine as a poet and writer—is vitally composed of the landscape within which we evolve as human cultural beings. Our

Existence is an equation that comprises what I have considered a mantra for some twenty-five years now: land, culture, and community.

A traditional religious ceremony recently took place at *Aacqu*. This is the seasonal time of the year when the spirit beings we call *kah-tzinah* are with our land, culture, and community for four days. They bring songs, dances, prayers, cultural knowledge (meditation), and material gifts of food, bread, fruit, nuts, pottery, baskets, cloth and fabric goods, and other traditional items that come from the bounty and natural resources of the *haatse*. They interact with the people as they have done since the beginning of cultural time. According to the world view of the *Aacqumeh hanoh*, the *kah-tzinah* that come to Aacqu are the powers of all creation. They are also the powers of lightning, thunder, and the rain needed to sustain the Earth and the countless forms of life it supports, which they bring from the sky and from those points in the universe that only they have access to and that we depend upon. Thus the ceremony is an experience of sustainability: land, culture, and community interacting with each other.

I was present at this recent ceremony. My grandchildren, ranging in age from infancy to young adulthood, were there, too, because this occasion is, in a real sense, especially for them as young tribal people, so that they will always know to live within the interactivity of sustainability.

All of these things come to mind when I read Jidi Majia's poem "Land" and I envision his words. *I deeply love the land around me,* he says in the first line. *I deeply love the land around me,* he repeats in the next stanza. And then in the final stanza, he repeats it one more time: *I love this land around me deeply.* Without land, culture, and community, we do not have a voice. So the poems composed by Jidi Majia in collaboration with his homeland are essentially and ultimately vital for the continuing Existence of the Nuosu and their land. And because of Jidi Majia's voice expressing his love of the land, I have to say to him, even though he is not with me in the immediate moment, *Hah-uh, ehmee-eh heh-yah tse dah-aah eh kah-aititah naatah dai Aacqu dzeh-she:* Yes, that is the reason why these ceremonies happen the way they do at this place of Acoma.

Poetry sustains us more than we realize. So in contemplation and honoring of *Rhapsody in Black* by Jidi Majia, Nuosu poet extraordinaire, I will share these words that I wrote some years ago:

> As we gather the gift of rain, with respectful and loving gratitude for its sustaining power, and as we drink water and wash with it and irrigate our orchards and gardens with it, we become part of that gift. The rain gathers us in an all-encompassing moment that we too often don't notice but is there all the time. And for that gathering, we are grateful.

I am extremely grateful for the visionary voice of Jidi Majia.

Simon J. Ortiz
July 29, 2013

TRANSLATOR'S NOTE

Right from the beginning of this project, I encountered concepts and perspectives that were fresh and challenging. One was the metaphorical range and resonance of the color black in the Nuosu world view; another was the way the physical landscape enters into Jidi Majia's poetic language; and yet another was the historical sense that emerges through trans-individual, tribal subjectivity.

The title of the collection sums up two important aspects of Jidi Majia as a poet. His work is rooted in the tribal traditions of his people, which he sums up with the word "blackness," partly because they call themselves the Nuosu ("Black Tribe"). At the same time, he embraces worldwide currents of thought, using a fluid succession of moods and reflections to express a modern sensibility (as in George Gershwin's *Rhapsody in Blue*).

In everything that Jidi Majia writes, there is this dual orientation: on one hand it is rooted in the land-based, tribal sensibility of the Nuosu, and on the other hand it is characterized by expansive subjectivity reaching out into the modern world. Although some poems convey an experience of being torn, Jidi Majia's primary labor of thought is aimed at integrating these two directions of thought.

The Nuosu are the most populous branch of the Yi people, a minority distributed in China's southwestern provinces and numbering over 7 million. Their language belongs to the Tibeto-Burman family, but unlike the Tibetans, they never embraced an outside belief system. They traditionally embraced a tapestry of beliefs: a sky god, a giant tiger as cosmogonic progenitor, nature spirits, sacred eagle ancestors, and epic heroes.

For the Nuosu people, blackness is the color of spiritual depth: it is a force that needs to be summoned up from deep within the land and the psyche. In "The Other Way" the poet writes: *"I see my other self pass through / The crown of darkness and duration / . . . I do not see his hand here before me / It is in the black depths of the land / It is holding up flowers of bone / So my tribe in its rituals will know / The presence of the ancestors' souls."* Thus blackness is a kind of gravitas that protects against curses and restless spiritual forces. Blackness is associated with nature's womblike potency, which engenders transient things. Hence it is also a zone of transformation, of surrender, of letting superficial impulses subside into cycles of natural life. These dimensions of the color are expressed in the title poem, in which Jidi Majia contemplates oncoming night as a kind of personal ceremony, entering into blackness as a zone of transformation and connectedness. As translator I have tried to engage sympathetically with blackness in all these senses.

The poet's connection to his tribal homeland is everywhere woven into his metaphoric language. In "Vigil for the *Bimo*," for example, a ritualist's death causes the language of Nuosu scriptures to become inaccessible. In the context of a topography where deforestation caused frequent mudslides, the land provides ready-to-hand metaphors for what happens to people on the land (and to their culture): "*When a* bimo *dies / The road of the native tongue is cut off by flash floods / All of its words, in an instant / Become pale and weak, their inherent meaning lost / Stories that once moved us / Solidify to stone . . .*" While translating this poem, I remembered a washed-out road from my visit to Zhaojue County, Sichuan. This remembered image prompted me to add a clarifying adjective—"by *flash* floods"—to appeal to the reader's topographic imagination.

In "Hometown Cremation Ground" the poet places group identity in a setting of vast time and space. One point of view is eternal—it is there with the sky. Another point of view is transient, belonging to one person's lifetime. There is also a river of awareness (a form of terrestrial cognition) that belongs to the collective suffering and struggle of the Nuosu tribe. Different temporal scales of awareness are embedded, one within the other: "*I know not when it was / My eyes were fastened / Onto the black dome of sky / With silent regard for thousands of years / Gazing upon this stretch of human ground / (In a faraway place / Through veils of mist / I catch sight of you / From my eyes a river flows).*" As translator I am fascinated by how the different scales of temporal awareness emerge one from the other. I think this relates to the poet's effort to have a dialogue with the history of his own people (an intention that he mentions in "One Kind of Voice"). There is no outside, objective, codified history backed up by academic "authority" here. Tribal history is subjective, intuitively carried along by the tribe's priests and poets down through time.

I cannot readily point to specific word choices that were influenced by my engagement with the Nuosu sensibility. The collected poems of Jidi Majia were my primary source for engaging with that sensibility. The poems have an infectious emotional current, and once I engaged with it, I felt it as a key driving force in my efforts to recast syntactic structures and find a fitting vatic register.

Denis Mair
July 2013
Gloaming Studio II, Seattle

POEMS

自画像

风在黄昏的山岗上悄悄对孩子说话，
风走了，远方有一个童话等着它。
孩子留下你的名字吧，在这块土地上，
因为有一天你会自豪地死去。

——题记

我是这片土地上用彝文写下的历史
是一个剪不断脐带的女人的婴儿
我痛苦的名字
我美丽的名字
我希望的名字
那是一个纺线女人
千百年来孕育着的
一首属于男人的诗
我传统的父亲
是男人中的男人
人们都叫他支呷阿鲁
我不老的母亲
是土地上的歌手
一条深沉的河流
我永恒的情人
是美人中的美人
人们都叫她呷玛阿妞
我是一千次死去
永远朝着左睡的男人
我是一千次死去
永远朝着右睡的女人
我是一千次葬礼开始后
那来自远方的友情
我是一千次葬礼高潮时
母亲喉头发颤的辅音

这一切虽然都包含了我
其实我是千百年来
正义和邪恶的抗争
其实我是千百年来
爱情和梦幻的儿孙
其实我是千百年来

SELF-PORTRAIT

> Wind blows over a ridge, speaking softly to a child at twilight. The wind goes off into the distance, where a tale awaits it. Leave your name on this land, child, for your time will come to die proudly.

I am history written on this land in the Nuosu tongue
I was born to a woman who could hardly bear to cut the birth cord
My pain-racked name
My beautiful name
My name full of hope
Is a poem of manhood
Gestated for a thousand years
By a woman at her spindle
My tradition-bearing father
Is a man among men
People call him Zhyge Alu*
My ageless mother
Is a singer upon this land
She is its deep-running river
My eternal beloved
Is a beauty among beauties
People call her Gamo Anyo**
In each of my thousand deaths as a man
I lay down to rest facing left
In each of my thousand deaths as a woman
I lay down to rest facing right
At the end of a thousand mourning rites
I am the kind words of a guest from afar
At the high point of a thousand mourning rites
I am a mother's quavering syllables

Though all of this includes me
In truth I am the millennial conflict
Of justice against evil
I am the millennial descendant
Of love and fantasy
Truly down through the centuries

---

* Zhyge Alu is a mythic hero of the Nuosu whose exploits are recounted in an epic of the same name.
** Gamo Anyo is a legendary Nuosu beauty.

一次没有完的婚礼
其实我是千百年来
一切背叛
一切忠诚
一切生
一切死
啊，世界，请听我回答
我—是—彝—人

All the mislaid wedding plans
Have been mine
All the treachery and loyalty
All the births and deaths
Have been mine
Ah world, let me give an answer
I—am—a—Nuosu!

回答

你还记得
那条通向吉勒布特 的小路吗?
一个流蜜的黄昏
她对我说:
我的绣花针丢了
快来帮我寻找
（我找遍了那条小路）

你还记得
那条通向吉勒布特的小路吗?
一个沉重的黄昏
我对她说:
那深深插在我心上的
不就是你的绣花针吗
（她感动地哭了）

ANSWER

Do you still remember
The little road to Jjile Bute?*
A honeyed twilight hour
She said to me:
I've lost my embroidery needle
Hurry up and help me find it
(I looked everywhere on that country lane)

Do you remember
The little road to Jjile Bute?
A heavy twilight hour
I said to her:
Something is stuck deep in my heart
Isn't that your embroidery needle?
(She was moved to tears)

---

* Jjile Bute is the poet's native place. The heartland of the Great Liangshan area, it is located in the Liangshan Yi Minority Autonomous Prefecture, Sichuan.

“睡”的和弦

如果森林是一片郁郁的海
他就沉沉地浮起
呼吸在海岸线上
小屋像一只船
搁浅在森林的最南方
搁浅在平原的最北方
抛锚在一个大港湾
猎狗弓着背打盹
为火塘以外的夜，画一个温热的
起伏的问号
他睡在那间
有女人的头发味和孩子的
奶香味的小屋里
那梦境似流水，诡秘地卷过
他朦胧的头顶
白日里那只母鹿漂亮的影子
刚从这里飘走
他开始追寻，肩上落满了
好多秋天的黄金叶
他没有开枪。他看见那只母鹿
在一座中国西南的山上跳舞
于是他也想跳
但妻子枕着他的左臂
孩子枕着他的右臂
这是两个小港湾
他好像只能用神思
吹着悠扬的口哨
走往日猎人那种细碎步
一首不尽的森林小夜曲
便从他的额头上悄悄滑过

THE CHORD OF "SLEEP"

If the forest is a sea of loden green
His weight is borne afloat there
And he breathes at the shoreline
In the boat of his hut
Beached at the southern edge of the forest
Beached at the northern edge of the plain
Run aground in a harbor
A curled-up hunting dog dozes
Like a cozy, heaving question mark
For the night beyond the stove's warmth
The man lies in the little room
Redolent of a woman's hair
And a child's milky breath
A dream-current slips in winding course
Past the obscured crown of his head
No sooner does the pretty shape
Of a doe glimpsed in daylight drift by
Than he gives pursuit, and onto his shoulders fall
Many golden leaves of autumn
He does not shoot the doe. He sees her
Dancing on a mountain in southwest China
Whereupon he too wants to dance
But his wife is pillowed on his left arm
His child is pillowed on his right arm
With these two coves on either side
It seems that only in spirit
Can he sound a long, haunting whistle
And tread the gliding step of old-time hunters
A forest nocturne that knows no end
Quietly slips past his forehead

彝人谈火

给我们血液，给我们土地
你比人类古老的历史还要漫长
给我们启示，给我们慰藉
让子孙在冥冥中，看见祖先的模样
你施以温情，你抚爱生命
让我们感受仁慈，理解善良
你保护着我们的自尊
免遭他人的伤害
你是禁忌，你是召唤，你是梦想
给我们无限的欢乐
让我们尽情地歌唱
当我们离开这个人世
你不会流露出丝毫的悲伤
然而无论贫穷，还是富有
你都会为我们的灵魂
穿上永恒的衣裳

A NUOSU SPEAKS OF FIRE

Give us blood, give us land
O power stretching beyond antiquity
Give us revelation, give us solace
Let the latter-born glimpse their forebears in a trance
You bestow warm care, you give succor to life
May we feel your benevolence, know your kindness
You have safeguarded our self-respect
Kept us from harm at others' hands
You are forbidden pleasure, you beckon to us in a dream
You give us limitless joy
You let us sing with abandon
When we leave the human world
Not a trace of sorrow will you show
Whether we lived in poverty or in wealth
You will dress our souls
In eternal garments of flame

反差

我没有目的

突然太阳在我的背后
预示着某种危险

我看见另一个我
穿过夜色和时间的头顶
吮吸苦荞的阴凉
我看见我的手不在这里
它在大地黑色的深处
高举着骨质的花朵
让仪式中的部族
召唤先祖们的灵魂

我看见一堵墙在阳光下古老
所有的谚语被埋进了酒中
我看见当音乐的节奏爬满羊皮
一个歌手用他飘忽着火焰的舌头
寻找超现实的土壤

我不在这里，因为还有另一个我
在朝着相反的方向走去

THE OTHER WAY

I have no goal

Suddenly the sun behind me
Warns of oncoming danger

I see my other self pass through
The crown of darkness and duration
Nursing on the coolness of buckwheat
I do not see his hand here before me
It is in the black depths of the land
It is holding up flowers of bone
So my tribe in its rituals will know
The presence of the ancestors' souls

I see an earthen wall, ancient under the sun
All proverbs have been preserved in wine
I see rhythms snaking over a drumhead
A singer loosens his flaming tongue
To seek surreal terrain

I am not here, for there is another one of me
Walking in an opposite direction

母亲们的手

> 彝人的母亲死了，在火葬的时候，她的身子永远是侧向右睡的，听人说那是因为，她还要用自己的左手，到神灵世界去纺线。
>
> ——题记

就这样向右悄悄地睡去
睡成一条长长的河流
睡成一架绵绵的山脉
许多人都看见了
她睡在那里
于是山的女儿和山的儿子们
便走向那看不见海的岸
岸上有一条美人鱼
当液态的土地沉下去
身后立起一块沉默的礁石
这时独有一支古老的歌曲
拖着一弯最纯洁的月牙

就这样向右悄悄地睡去
在清清的风中
在濛濛的雨里
让淡淡的雾笼罩
让白白的云萦绕
无论是在静静的黎明
还是在迷人的黄昏
一切都成了冰冷的雕像
只有她的左手还漂浮着
皮肤上一定有温度
血管里一定有血流

就这样向右悄悄地睡去
多么像一条美人鱼
多么像一弯纯洁的月牙
多么像一块沉默的礁石
她睡在土地和天空之间
她睡在死亡和生命的高处
因此江河才在她身下照样流着
因此森林才在她身下照样长着
因此山岩才在她身下照样站着

MOTHER'S HAND

Among the Nuosu, when a mother dies, her body is laid out facing rightward to be cremated. People say this leaves her left hand free so that she can continue spinning yarn even in the spirit world.

In this right-facing pose she goes off to sleep
The sleep of a long river
The sleep of a far-stretching ridgeline
Many people have seen her
Laid out in those places
Whereupon those highland sons and daughters
Go to the shore of an unseen ocean
And where the waves of land subside
A mermaid remains on the shore
Behind her is a brooding shoal
Where only an ancient song is heard
Bearing up the purest of crescent moons

In this right-facing pose she goes off to sleep
In the clear-aired wind
In a hazy rain shower
She is enveloped in thin mist
She is enwreathed in white clouds
Whether at tranquil daybreak
Or at enchanting twilight
All else turns to chilled sculpture
Only her left arm floats free
Its skin surely gives off warmth
Its veins surely flow with blood

In this right-facing pose she goes off to sleep
How like a mermaid she is
How like a crescent moon
How like a brooding shoal
She sleeps between land and sky
She sleeps on the heights of birth and death
Only thus do rivers keep flowing beneath her
Only thus do forests keep growing beneath her
Only thus do boulders keep standing beneath her

因此我苦难而又甜蜜的民族
才这样哭着，才这样喊着，才这样唱着

就这样向右悄悄地睡去
世间的一切都要消失
在浩瀚的苍穹中
在不死的记忆里
只有她的左手还漂浮着
那么温柔，那么美丽，那么自由

Only thus do my sweet, suffering people
Keep weeping and shouting and singing

In this right-facing pose she goes off to sleep
All things in the world will fade away
In the vast vault of heaven
In undying memory
Only her left arm still floats
So tender, so beautiful and free

听《送魂经》

要是在活着的日子
就能请毕摩为自己送魂
要是在活着的日子
就能沿着祖先的路线回去
要是这一切
都能做到
而不是梦想
要是我那些
早已长眠的前辈
问我每天在干些什么
我会如实地说
这个家伙
热爱所有的种族
以及女子的芳唇
他还常常在夜里写诗
但从未坑害过人

LISTENING TO THE SOUL-SENDING SCRIPTURE

If I could ask a *bimo* to send off my soul*
During the days of my lifetime
If I could trace the route back to my ancestors
During the days of my lifetime
If all this could be done
And were not a dream
And if my elders who have gone
To their eternal rest
Were to ask me what I do each day
I would say truthfully
This fellow has ardent love
For all races of people
And for the fragrant lips of women
He often stays up late writing poems
But he has never done harm to others

---

* A *bimo* is a ritualist, scholar, and culture-bearer of the Nuosu people. In Nuosu villages, one often comes upon a *bimo* chanting from a rolled-up scripture written on leather or papyrus-like material. A *bimo* characteristically wears a conical hat of black felt and a cape of black wool.

古里拉达的岩羊

再一次瞩望
那奇妙的境界
其实一切都在天上
通往神秘的永恒
从这里连接无边的浩瀚
空虚和寒冷就在那里
蹄子的回声沉默

雄性的弯角
装饰远走的云雾
背后是黑色的深渊
它那童贞的眼睛
泛起幽蓝的波浪

在我的梦中
不能没有这颗星星
在我的灵魂里
不能没有这道闪电
我怕失去了它
在大凉山的最高处
我的梦想会化为乌有

MOUNTAIN GOATS OF GUNYILADA

Again I survey the vista
Of that marvelous domain
In truth it is in the sky realm
It opens out onto vastness
It leads somewhere magical and timeless
In that place of emptiness and cold
Echoes of hooves fade into silence

The crescent horns of the male
Are set off against a scudding cloud
And behind it is a black abyss
Its childlike eyes stir
Like blue elusive waves

Within my dreams
I cannot do without this star
Within my soul
I cannot do without this lightning flash
I fear that if it is lost
From the heights of Greater Liangshan
My dreams will dissolve to nothing

部落的节奏

在充满宁静的时候
我也能察觉
它掀起的欲望
爬满了我的灵魂
引来一阵阵风暴

在自由漫步的时候
我也能感到
它激发的冲动
奔流在我的体内
想驱赶一双腿
去疯狂地迅跑

在甜蜜安睡的时候
我也能发现
它牵出的思念
萦绕在我的大脑
让梦终夜地失眠

呵，我知道
多少年来
就是这种神奇的力量
它让我的右手
在淡淡的忧郁中
写下了关于彝人的诗行

RHYTHM OF A TRIBE

In moments of tranquility
I can also detect
The desire it stirs
Snaking through my soul
Bringing on storms

Even when I stroll at ease
I still have a sense
Of its energizing impulse
Coursing inside my body
Trying to goad my legs
Into making a mad dash

At times of sweet slumber
I notice it tugging at my thoughts
Until they coil in my brain
Filling the night with restless dreams

Ah, I also know
All these years
It has been this marvelous force
In a state of slight melancholy
That makes my right hand
Write down poems about the Nuosu

土地

我深深地爱着这片土地
不只因为我们在这土地生
不只因为我们在这土地死
不只因为有那么多古老的家谱
我们见过面和没有见过面的亲人
都在这块土地上一个又一个地逝去
不只因为在这土地上
有着我们千百条深沉的野性的河流
祖先的血液在日日夜夜地流淌

我深深地爱着这片土地
不只因为那些如梦的古歌
在人们的心里是那样的悲凉
不只因为在这土地上
妈妈的抚摸是格外的慈祥
不只因为在这土地上
有着我们温暖的瓦板屋
千百年来为我们纺着线的
是那些坐在低矮的木门前
死去了的和至今还活着的祖母
不只因为在这土地上
我们的古磨还在黄昏时分歌唱
那金黄的醉人的温馨
流进了每一个女人黝黑的乳房

我深深地爱着这片土地
还因为它本身就是那样的平平常常
无论我怎样地含着泪对它歌唱
它都沉默得像一块岩石一声不响
只有在我悲哀和痛苦的时候
当我在这土地的某一个地方躺着
我就会感到土地——这彝人的父亲
在把一个沉重的摇篮轻轻地摇晃

LAND

I deeply love the land around me
Not only because we are born on this land
Not only because we die on this land
Not only for all the ancient family trees
Our relations we have seen and have not seen
Who one by one have passed away on this land
Not only because this land is crossed
By hundreds of deep-set wild rivers
And ancestral blood trickles night by night

I deeply love the land around me
Not only because of dreamy old songs
That strike the heart with such sorrow
Not only because a mother's caress
Carries an extra measure of kindness
Not only because this land holds
Our warm tile-roofed cottages
For centuries our yarn has been spun
By women who sit at low wooden doors
Those now dead and the grandmother still living
Not only because of the ancient millstone
That still hums at dusk on this land
Suffusing the air with a rich amber scent
Seeping into each woman's dark breasts

I love this land around me deeply
Simply for what it is on ordinary days
No matter how tearfully we sing to it
It remains as wordless as a boulder
Yet in times of sorrow and suffering
When we lie down at a certain spot
We feel this land—father of the Nuosu
Lightly rocking us in its heavy cradle

黑色狂想曲

在死亡和生命相连的梦想之间
在河流和土地的幽会之处
当星星以睡眠的姿态
在蓝色的夜空静默
当歌手忧郁的嘴唇失去柔软
木门不再响动，石磨不再歌唱
摇篮曲的最后一个音符跳跃成萤火
所有疲倦的母亲都已进入梦乡

而在远方，在云的后面
在那山岩的最高点
沉睡的鹰爪踏着梦想的边缘
死亡在那个遥远的地方紧闭着眼
而在远方，在这土地上
千百条河流在月光下游动
它们的影子走向虚无
而在远方，在那森林里
在松针诱惑的枕头旁
残酷的豹忘记了吞食身边的岩羊
在这寂静的时刻
啊，古里拉达峡谷中没有名字的河流
请给我你血液的节奏
让我的口腔成为你的声带

大凉山男性的乌抛山
快去拥抱小凉山女性的阿呷居木山
让我的躯体再一次成为你们的胚胎
让我在你腹中发育
让那已经消失的记忆重新膨胀

在这寂静的时刻
啊，黑色的梦想，你快覆盖我，笼罩我
让我在你情人般的抚摸中消失吧

RHAPSODY IN BLACK

Among dreams, where life and death are joined
Where soil and rivers have their rendezvous
When somnolent stars beam in silence
In the deep-blue sky of night
When the singer's lips are set in a pensive line
The wooden door does not creak, the millstone does not hum
The lullaby's last notes leap up like fireflies
And all weary mothers have entered dreamland

Far away on the other side of the clouds
Atop the highest crag
Eagle talons tread on a dream's edge
And here, in *this* faraway land
Where the eyes of death are sealed
Hundreds of rivers race beneath moonlight
Their forms head off toward nothingness
And far away in the forest
Next to tempting pine-needle pillows
The panther no longer preys on the mountain goat
In this moment of stillness
O nameless river in the chasm of Gunyilada
Give me the rhythm of your lifeblood
Let the roof of my mouth resound with your voice

Oh, hurry, male mountain Vupuo of the Greater Liangshan range
Embrace the female mountain Agajjumu of Lesser Liangshan
Let my body be your embryo once again
Let me gestate in your womb
Let vanished memory swell again

Ah black dream, at this silent moment
May you soon cover me, envelop me*
Let me disappear under your lover-like touch

---

* In the Nuosu worldview, blackness is associated with a power that lies deep within the soil and within the soul. Though it reposes in the deepest places, it is paradoxically the most elevated power. In normal times it is not fully in evidence, so it needs to be invoked or otherwise brought forth. Once manifested, it has gravitas and unifying force that can overcome superficial, restless spiritual forces. Thus the power of blackness is able to banish demons. The power of blackness makes things merge together, and anything that entered it can come out in a new form. Here the poet borrows the covering darkness of night as a metaphor for this fundamental blackness. For a discussion of blackness in the Nuosu worldview, see Luo Qingchun 罗庆春, *Shenwu de zhuzhou* 神巫的祝咒 (Beijing: Zhongguo xiju Press, 2012).

让我成为空气，成为阳光
成为岩石，成为水银，成为女贞子
让我成为铁，成为铜
成为云母，成为石棉，成为磷火
啊，黑色的梦想，你快吞没我，溶化我
让我在你仁慈的保护下消失吧
让我成为草原，成为牛羊
成为獐子，成为云雀，成为细鳞鱼
让我成为火镰，成为马鞍
成为口弦，成为马布，成为卡谢着尔
啊，黑色的梦想，就在我消失的时候
请为我弹响悲哀和死亡之琴吧
让吉狄马加这个痛苦而又沉重的名字
在子夜时分也染上太阳神秘的色彩

让我的每一句话，每一支歌
都是这土地灵魂里最真实的回音
让我的每一句诗，每一个标点
都是从这土地蓝色的血管里流出
啊，黑色的梦想，就在我消失的时候
请让我对着一块巨大的岩石说话
身后是我苦难而又崇高的人民
我深信这千年的孤独和悲哀呵
要是岩石听懂了也会淌出泪来
啊，黑色的梦想，就在我消失的时候
请为我的民族升起明亮而又温暖的星星吧
啊，黑色的梦想，让我伴随着你
最后进入那死亡之乡

Let me turn into air, into sunlight
Into boulders and quicksilver and privet flowers
Let me turn into iron, into bronze
Into pearly shells, into asbestos, into phosphor
Ah black dream, may you soon engulf and dissolve me
Let me vanish under your benign protection
To become a grassland and its herds
To become a muntjac or a lark or a fine-scaled fish
To become a firestone, to become a saddle
To become a mouth harp or a *mabu* or a *kaxi-jjuhli**
Ah black dream, as I fade away
Pluck lute strings of sorrow and death for me
Let the pain-racked, burdened name Jidi Majia
Be tinged by the sun's spectral colors, even at midnight

Let every word I speak, each song I sing
Give truest voice to the spirit in this soil
Let each line of poetry, each punctuation mark
Flow forth from the blue veins of this soil
Ah black dream, just as I disappear
Let me converse with a monolith of rock
With my suffering, high-minded people behind me
I trust that their centuries of lonely sorrow
Were it heard, would draw tears from a boulder
Ah black dream, just as I disappear
Let the bright, warm star of my people rise
Ah black dream, let me follow you
To enter death's country at last

---

* The *mabu* and *kaxi-jjuhly* are musical instruments used by the Nuosu.

岩石

它们有着彝族人的脸形
生活在群山最孤独的地域
这些似乎没有生命的物体
黝黑的前额爬满了鹰爪的痕迹
（当岁月漫溢的情感
穿过了所有的虚幻的季节
望着古老的天空和熟悉的大地
无边的梦想，迷离的回忆
只有那阳光燃成的火焰
让它们接近于死亡的睡眠
可是谁又能告诉我呢？
这一切包含了人类的不幸）

我看见过许多没有生命的物体
它们有着彝族人的脸形
一个世纪又一个世纪的沉默
并没有把他们的痛苦减轻

BOULDERS

They are shaped like the faces of Nuosu people
Who live in the loneliest mountain regions
These seemingly lifeless objects
Swarthy brows scrabbled with marks of eagle talons
(When the feelings of the years overflow
And pass through all the illusory seasons
Unbounded dreams and stray memories
Survey the ageless sky and soil
Only after the sun's fire has kindled them
Can they approach the sleep of death
But who can tell me what human misfortunes
Are contained in all this)

I have seen many lifeless objects
That are shaped like the faces of Nuosu people
Century after century of silence
Has done nothing to ease their agony

群山的影子

跟随太阳而来
命运的使者
没有头
没有嘴
没有骚动和喧哗

它是光的羽衣
来自隐秘的地方
抚摸倦意和万物的渴望
并把无名的预感
传给就要占卜的羊骨

那是自由的灵魂
彝人的护身符
躺在它宁静的怀中
可以梦见黄昏的星辰
淡忘钢铁的声音

SHADE OF MOUNTAINS

Following the sun it comes
Harbinger of fate
It has no head or mouth
It makes no disturbance or fanfare

It trails a feathered cape of light
From a hidden place emerging
To comfort the weariness and longing of all beings
And to the sheep's knuckles a diviner will throw
It imparts a nameless presentiment

This is the spirit of freedom
The talisman that guards the Nuosu people
Those who lie in its quiet embrace
Will dream of stars coming out at dusk
Will find respite from screeching steel

故土的神灵

把自己的脚步放轻
穿过自由的森林
让我们同野兽一道行进
让我们陷入最初的神秘

不要惊动它们
那些岩羊、獐子和花豹
它们是白雾忠实的儿子
伴着微光悄悄地隐去

不要打扰永恒的平静
在这里到处都是神灵的气息
死了的先辈正从四面走来
他们惧怕一切不熟悉的阴影

把脚步放轻，还要放轻
尽管命运的目光已经爬满了绿叶
往往在这样异常沉寂的时候
我们会听见来自另一个世界的声音

SPIRITS OF THE OLD LAND

Lighten your footsteps
To pass through freedom's forest
Let us advance in company with wild beasts
Let us plunge into the original mystery

Do not startle them
Those mountain goats, river deer, and panthers
Those faithful children of the white mist
Stealing away among pale wisps

Do not disturb the eternal stillness
An air of divine presences is all around
Departed elders draw near on all sides
They are fearful of unfamiliar shadows

Walk with light footsteps, still lighter
Though fate's glance may be overgrown with greenery
Often at this time of utter stillness
We hear the sounds of another world

苦荞麦

荞麦啊，你无声无息
你是大地的容器
你在吮吸星辰的乳汁
你在回忆白昼炽热的光
荞麦啊，你把自己根植于
土地生殖力最强的部位
你是原始的隐喻和象征
你是高原滚动不安的太阳
荞麦啊，你充满了灵性
你是我们命运中注定的方向
你是古老的语言
你的倦意是徐徐来临的梦想
只有通过你的祈祷
我们才能把祝愿之辞
送到神灵和先辈的身边
荞麦啊，你看不见的手臂
温柔而修长，我们
渴望你的抚摸，我们歌唱你
就如同歌唱自己的母亲一样

BITTER BUCKWHEAT

Buckwheat, you make no sound
You vessel of the earth's richness
You are drinking the milk of starlight
As you remember the blazing light of day
Buckwheat, you push your roots down
Into the land's most fertile zone
You are a primal metaphor and symbol
You are the roiling sun of the highlands
Buckwheat, you are full of spirit-nature
You are the direction ordained in our fate
You are an ancient language
Your fatigue is an encroachment of dreams
You are the only prayer by which
Our invocation can reach the side
Of nature spirits and ancestors
Buckwheat, your invisible arms
Are tender and long
We yearn for your caress and sing of you
Just as we sing of our own mothers

看不见的人

在一个神秘的地点
有人在喊我的名字
但我不知道
这个人是谁?
我想把它的声音带走
可是听来却十分生疏
我敢肯定
在我的朋友中
没有一个人曾这样喊叫我

在一个神秘的地点
有人在写我的名字
但我不知道
这个人是谁?
我想在梦中找到它的字迹
可是醒来总还是遗忘
我敢肯定
在我的朋友中
没有一个人曾这样写信给我

在一个神秘的地点
有人在等待我
但我不知道
这个人是谁?
我想透视一下它的影子
可是除了虚无什么也没有
我敢肯定
在我的朋友中
没有一个人曾这样跟随我

SOMEONE UNSEEN

In a mysterious place
Someone is calling my name
But I do not know
Who it might be
I want to carry his voice with me
But it is unfamiliar to my ear
I can affirm
That among my friends
No one has called me this way

In a mysterious place
Someone is writing my name
But I do not know
Who it might be
I try to construe his writing in dreams
But on waking I always forget it
I can definitely say
That among my friends
No one has written me such a letter

In a mysterious place
Someone is waiting for me
But I do not know
Who this person might be
I wish to fix my gaze on his silhouette
But aside from emptiness there is nothing
I can definitely say
That among my friends
No one has followed me this way

守望毕摩

——献给彝人中的祭司

毕摩死的时候
母语像一条路被洪水切断
所有的词，在瞬间
变得苍白无力，失去了本身的意义
曾经感动过我们的故事
被凝固成石头，沉默不语

守望毕摩
就是守望一种文化
就是守望一个启示
其实我们没有选择的余地
因为时间已经证实
就在他渐渐消隐的午后
传统似乎已经被割裂
史诗的音符变得冰凉

守望毕摩
我们悼念的不但是
一个民族的心灵
我们的两眼泪水剔透
那是在为智慧和精神的死亡
而哀伤

守望毕摩
是对一个时代的回望
那里有多少神秘、温情和泪水啊！

VIGIL FOR THE *BIMO*

—Dedicated to a Nuosu ritualist

When a *bimo* dies
The road of the native tongue is cut off by flash floods
All of its words, in an instant
Become pale and weak, their inherent meaning lost
Stories that once moved us
Solidify to stone, subside into silence

To keep vigil for a *bimo*
Is to keep vigil for a culture
Is to keep vigil for what edified us
Because time has already proven
That in fact we have no room for choice
On the afternoon he faded away
It seemed as if tradition had been torn apart
The notes of an epic turned icy

Keeping vigil for a *bimo*
We are not only mourning
For the inner essence of one people
Our eyes shimmer with tears
Because we grieve for departed wisdom
And for the life of the mind

To keep vigil for a *bimo*
Is retrospection of an era
It was so rich in mystery, affection, and tears!

毕摩的声音

——献给彝人中的祭司之二

你听见它的时候
它就在梦幻之上
如同一缕淡淡的青烟
为什么群山在这样的时候
才充满着永恒的寂静
这是谁的声音？它漂浮在人鬼之间
似乎已经远离了人的躯体
然而它却在真实与虚无中
同时用人和神的口说出了
生命与死亡的赞歌
当它呼喊太阳、星辰、河流和英雄的祖先
召唤神灵与超现实的力量
死去的生命便开始了复活！

VOICE OF THE *BIMO*

—Dedicated to a Nuosu ritualist

When you hear it
It seems above all illusion
Like a faint wisp of bluish smoke
Why just now are the ranged mountains
Felt to be filled with a timeless stillness?
Whose voice drifts between men and ghosts?
It seems to have left the body
Yet between reality and nothingness
In tones both human and divine, it utters
A praise song for birth and death
When it invokes sun, stars, rivers, and ancient heroes
When it summons deities and surreal powers
Departed beings commence their resurrection!

星回节的祝愿

我祝愿蜜蜂
我祝愿金竹，我祝愿大山
我祝愿活着的人们
避开不幸的灾难
长眠的祖先
到另一个世界平安
我祝愿这片土地
它是母亲的身躯
哪怕就是烂醉如泥
我也无法忘记

我祝愿凡是种下的玉米
都能生出美丽的珍珠
我祝愿每一头绵羊
都像约呷哈且 那样勇敢
我祝愿每一只公鸡
都像瓦补多几 那样雄健
我祝愿每一匹赛马
都像达里阿左那样驰名
我祝愿太阳永远不灭
火塘更加温暖
我祝愿森林中的獐子
我祝愿江河里的游鱼
神灵啊，我祝愿
因为你不会不知道
这是彝人最真实的情感

WISHES FOR THE FESTIVAL OF RETURNING STARS*

I offer wishes for honeybees
For golden bamboo and the great mountains
I offer wishes that we the living
Can be spared any terrible disasters
And that the ancestors who have gone to eternal rest
Will arrive at peace in the other world
I offer wishes for this expanse of land
Which is our mother's body
Even if I were falling-down drunk
I could not possibly forget

May each seed of corn that is planted
Grow into beautiful pearls
May every sheep turn out as bold
As the lead ram Yogga-hxaqie**
May every rooster be as formidable
As the fighting cock Vabu-dajy***
May every swift-footed horse
Win the fame of Dalie-azho****
May the sun never be extinguished
May the fireplace burn warmer
I offer wishes for roe deer in the forest
And for fish swimming in the rivers
Spirits of the land, I make these wishes
Being confident that you surely know
This feeling is closest to a Nuosu's heart

* The "Festival of Returning Stars" is another name for *Du-zi*, the "Torch Festival" of the Nuosu.
** Yogga-hxaqie is a fearless lead ram, or bellwether, mentioned in Nuosu songs and tales.
*** Vabu-dajy is a famous fighting rooster mentioned in Nuosu tales.
**** Dalie-azho is a famous racehorse in Nuosu stories.

布拖女郎

就是从她那古铜般的脸上
我第一次发现了那片土地的颜色
我第一次发现了太阳鹅黄色的眼泪
我第一次发现了那季风留下的齿痕
我第一次发现了幽谷永恒的沉默

就是从她那谜一样动人的眼里
我第一次听到了高原隐隐的雷声
我第一次听见了黄昏轻推着木门
我第一次听见了火塘甜蜜的叹息
我第一次听见了头巾下如水的吻

就是从她那安然平静的额前
我第一次看见了远方风暴的缠绵
我第一次看见了岩石盛开着花朵
我第一次看见了梦着情人的月光
我第一次看见了四月怀孕的河流

就是从她那倩影消失的地方
我第一次感到了悲哀和孤独
但我永远不会忘记那一天
在大凉山一个多雨的早晨
一个孩子的初恋被带到了远方

BUTUO LASS

It was from the bronze of her complexion
That I first discovered the color of the land around me
I first discovered the pale yellow tears of the sun
I first discovered the teeth marks of seasonal winds
I first discovered the timeless quiet of a glen

It was from the touching riddle of her eyes
That I first heard the muted thunder of the highlands
I first heard dusk push open a wooden door
I first heard the sweet sigh of a fireplace
I first heard a watery kiss beneath a headscarf

It was from her calm, placid forehead
That I first saw twining currents in a storm front
I first saw boulders bloom with lush flowers
I first saw how the moon dreams of her lover
I first saw a pregnant river in April

It was from something about her that has faded
That I first felt real sorrow and loneliness
But I will never forget the day
In Greater Liangshan, on a rainy morning
A child's first love was taken to far places

题辞

——献给我的汉族保姆

就是这个女人，这个年轻时
曾经无比美丽的村姑，这个
十六岁时就不幸被人奸淫了的女子
这个只身一人越过金沙江
又越过大渡河，到过大半个旧中国的女人
就是这个女人，受过许多磨难，而又从不
被人理解，在不该死去丈夫的年龄成了寡妇
就是这个女人，后来又结了婚
可那个男人要小她二十岁
最终她还是为这个男人吃尽了苦头
就是这个女人，历尽了人世沧桑和冷暖
但她却时时刻刻都梦想着一个世界
那里，充满着甜蜜和善良，充满着人性和友爱
就是这个女人，我在她的怀里度过了童年
我在她的身上和灵魂里，第一次感受到了
那超越了一切种族的、属于人类最崇高的情感
就是这个女人，是她把我带大成人
并使我相信，人活在世上都是兄弟
（尽管千百年来那些可怕的阴影
也曾深深地伤害过我）

那一天她死去了，脸上挂着迷人的微笑
岁月的回忆在她眼里变得无限遥远
而这一切都将成为永恒
诚然大地并没有因为失去这样一个平凡的
女人
感到过真正的颤栗和悲哀
但在大凉山，一个没有音乐的黄昏
她的彝人孩子将会为她哭泣
整个世界都会听见这忧伤的声音

INSCRIBED IN A MEMORIAL VOLUME

—Dedicated to my nanny of the Han nationality

This was a woman who in her girlhood
Was the unrivaled beauty of her village
This was a maiden who was molested at sixteen
Who crossed the Jinsha River alone, and then the Dadu
Whose tracks covered half of old China
This woman was put through trials and sadly misunderstood
She had to endure untimely widowhood
And then marry someone twenty years her junior
In the end she endured much bitterness for him
The world dealt out its coldest twists of fate to her
But she always dreamed of another kind of world
Filled with sweet kindness and human ties
In this woman's arms I spent my childhood
From her body and soul I sensed fellowship beyond race
This woman reared me to adulthood
She convinced me that the world's people are brothers
(Though the dark legacy of centuries
Had deeply wounded my soul)

The day she died, her charming smile remained on her face
The memories she held close receded from her sight
Yet what she stood for will never fade
In truth the good earth neither grieved nor trembled
Over the loss of this ordinary woman, but in Greater Liangshan
On an ordinary evening with no music
Her Nuosu child weeps for her
The world will hear this sorrowful sound

远山

我想听见吉勒布特的高腔
妈妈，我什么时候才能回到你身旁
我想到那个人的声浪里去
让我沉重的四肢在甜蜜中摇晃

我要横穿十字路口，我要越过密集的红灯
我不会理睬
那些警察的呼叫
我要击碎那阻挡我的玻璃门窗
我不会介意
鲜血凝成的花朵将在我渴望的双手开放
我要选择最近的道路
我要用头碰击那钢筋水泥的高层建筑
我要撞开那混杂的人流
我不会害怕
那冷漠而憎恶的目光降落在我湿淋淋的背后

我要跳过无数的砖墙
迅跑起来如同荒原的风
我要爬上那最末一辆通往山里的汽车
尽管我的一只脚，已经完全麻木
它被挤压在锈迹斑斑的车门上

最终我要轻轻地抚摸
脚下那多情而沉默的土地
我要赤裸着，好似一个婴儿
就像在母亲的怀里一样
我要看见我所有的梦想
在瓦板屋顶寂静的黄昏时分
全都伸出一双美丽的手掌
然后从我的额头前，悄悄地赶走
那些莫名的淡淡的忧伤

FAR MOUNTAINS

I love to hear the high-toned songs of Jjile Bute*
Mother, when can I return to your side?
I wish to enter the singer's stream of sound
Let my heavy limbs sway in that sweetness

I will jaywalk the intersections, run the gauntlet of red lights
I will pay no heed
To policemen's shouts
I will smash through glass partitions in my way
I will pay no mind to blood-clot flowers
Opening in my impatient hands
I will select the shortest route
I will butt against steel and concrete high-rises
I will knock the milling human stream aside
I will not fear the cold, invidious glances
That fall on my sweat-drenched back

I will jump over countless brick walls
Run like wind in a wasteland
I will climb onto the last bus to the mountains
I will cram my way in, despite the numbness
Of my leg caught in the rust-speckled door

At last my gentle steps will caress
The loving land that sleeps underfoot
I will be naked like a newborn baby
Held in his mother's arms
In the quiet hour of dusk over tile roofs
I will see all my dreams as one
Reaching two beautiful hands
Toward my forehead, to brush away
My nameless pall of sadness

* In Jjile Bute, folk songs are sung in a strongly emotive, high-pitched style.

白色的世界

我知道，我知道
死亡的梦想
只有一个色调
白色的牛羊
白色的房屋和白色的山岗
我知道，我真的知道
就是
迷幻中的苦荞
也像白雪一样

毕摩告诉我
你的祖先
都在那里幸福地流浪
在那个世界上
没有烦恼，没有忧愁
更没有阴谋和暗害
一条白色的道路
可以通向永恒的向往

啊，原谅我
在这悲哀的世纪，我承认过
幻想超过了现实的美妙
可是今天我还是要说
人啊，应该善良
活着本身就不容易
我热爱生命和这片土地
并不是因为我惧怕死亡

WHITE WORLD

I know, yes, I know
The dream of death
Has only a single color
Cows and sheep are white
Houses and mountains are white
I know, truly I know
Even the phantasmal buckwheat
Has a snowy whiteness

The *bimo* tells me of my ancestors
Who roam there in felicity
There is nothing to vex them
In that world, no moody cares
No foul plots and treachery
A white-colored road will lead us
To that place eternally longed for

Ah, forgive me, in this tragic world I do confess
To fantasies of beauty beyond the real
But to speak of what I feel today
Being human, we should be kind
Just living our lives is not easy
I have a passion for life on this land
Not because I fear where death may take me

看不见的波动

有一种东西，在我
出生之前
它就存在着
如同空气和阳光
有一种东西，在血液之中奔流
但是用一句话
的确很难说清楚
有一种东西，早就潜藏在
意识的最深处
回想起来却有模糊
有一种东西，虽然不属于现实
但我完全相信
鹰是我们的父亲
而祖先走过的路
肯定还是白色
有一种东西，恐怕已经成了永恒
时间稍微一长
就是望着终日相依的群山
自己的双眼也会潮湿
有一种东西，让我默认
万物都有灵魂，人死了
安息在土地和天空之间
有一种东西，似乎永远不会消失
如果作为一个彝人
你还活在世上！

AN INVISIBLE WAVE

A kind of thing
that existed
before my birth
and that exists
as air and sunlight do
A kind of thing that runs in my blood
yet cannot be explained
in so many words
A kind of thing, hidden early on
in depths of consciousness
Looking back, it seems obscure
A kind of thing, though not part of reality
That I have assurance of
The eagle was our father
The road our ancestors walked
Was assuredly white
A kind of thing that, I think, has become eternal
Take some time just to gaze
At ranged mountains, standing by each other
And your own eyes will moisten
A kind of thing that lets me acknowledge
All living things have souls, and the one who dies
Goes to rest between earth and sky
A kind of thing, it seems, that will never disappear
If you are still alive
As a Nuosu in this world!

故乡的火葬地

不知是什么时候
我的眼睛被钉在
那黑色的天幕的板上
它用千年的沉默和爱恋
注视着这片人性的土地
（在一个遥远的地方
穿过那沉重的迷雾
我望见了你
我的眼睛里面流出了河流）

我听见远古的风
在这土地上最后消失
我听见一支古老的歌曲
从人的血液里流出后
在这土地上凝固成神奇的岩石
我看见那些早已死去的亲人
在这土地上无声地汇聚
他们紧抱着彼此的影子
发出金属断裂的声音
我看见那些
早已死去的亲人的灵魂
在这土地上游来游去
像一条自由的黑色的鲸
（在一个遥远的地方
穿过那沉重的迷雾
我望见了你
我的眼睛里面流出了河流）

当然总会有这么一天
我的灵魂也会飞向
这片星光下的土地
像一只疲惫的鸟
向着最后的陆地奔去
那时我这彝人的头颅
将和祖先们的头颅靠在一起
用那最古老的彝语
诉说对往昔的思念
那时我们将仰着头
用空洞的眼睛
望着那永恒而又迷乱的星空
用那无形的嘴倾诉

HOMETOWN CREMATION GROUND

I know not when it was
My eyes were fastened
Onto the black dome of sky
With silent regard for thousands of years
Gazing upon this stretch of human ground
(In a faraway place
Through veils of mist
I catch sight of you
From my eyes a river flows)

I listen to a faraway wind
That dies away on this land at last
I hear a snatch of ancient song
Having flowed forth from human blood
It hardened to a wondrous boulder on this land
I see my long-dead relations
In silent assembly on this land
Embracing each other's shadows
Making sounds of screeching metal
I see the souls of dead loved ones
Swimming here and there on this land
Like black whales moving freely
(In a faraway place
Through a veil of mist
I catch sight of you
From my eyes a river flows)

Of course, there will come a day
My soul will also wing its way
To that stretch of ground beneath the stars
Like a weary bird that pushes onward
To that last piece of solid ground
Whereupon this Nuosu skull of mine
Will rest against my ancestors' skulls
And use the ancient Nuosu tongue
To tell how much I miss the past
At which time our turned-up heads
Will gaze with hollow eyes
At the eternal puzzle of starry skies
And with invisible lips will tell

人的善良和人的友爱
如果这大地上
还会传来一点回声
只要那是人的声音
我们就立刻在这土地上
让灵魂甜蜜地长眠
（在一个遥远的地方
穿过那沉重的迷雾
我望见了你
我的眼睛里面流出了河流）

Of kindness and fellow feeling
If even the slightest echo
Still sounds upon the good earth
And if only there be a human voice
Still present on this good earth
We will go to our sweet eternal rest
(In a faraway place
Through a veil of mist
I catch sight of you
From my eyes a river flows)

太阳

望着太阳，我便想
从它的光线里
去发现和惊醒我的祖先
望着太阳，大声说话
让它真正听见
并把这种神秘的语言
告诉那些灵魂
望着太阳，尽管我
常被人误解和中伤
可我还是相信
人更多的还是属于善良
望着太阳，是多么的美妙
季节在自己的皮肤上
漾起看不见的晚潮
望着太阳，总会去思念
因为在更早的时候
有人曾感受过它的温暖
但如今他们却不在这个世上

SUN

Looking at the sun, I wish
With the help of its rays
To discover and rouse my ancestors
Looking at the sun, I speak loudly
In a way they can hear
I address their souls
In my own mystical language
Looking at the sun, though I am wounded
And have not been understood by others
Still I believe
Most people belong to the good side
Looking at the sun, how wonderful it is
The invisible tide of the season laps
Against my bronze skin
Looking at the sun always makes me miss
Those people before my time
Who once could feel this warmth
And are no longer in this world

致布拖少女

你细长的脖子
能赛过阿呷查莫鸟的
美丽颈项
你的眼睛是湖水倒映的星光
你的前额如同金子
浮悬着蜜蜂的记忆
你高高的银质领箍
是一块网织的悬岩
你神奇多姿的裙裾
在黄昏退潮的时候
为夜的来临尽情摆浪
你那光滑的肌肤
恰似初夏的风穿越撒满松针的幽谷
然后悄悄地掠过母羊的腹部

你的呼吸回旋如梦幻
万物在你的鼻息下
摇动一颗颗金色的晨露
你的笑声
起伏就像天上的云雀
可以断定
因为你的舞步
山脉的每一次碰撞
牛角的每一次冲动
都预示着秋天的成熟

TO A BUTUO GIRL

Your slender neck outdoes in beauty
The neck of an *agachamo* bird*
Your eyes resemble stars reflected on a lake
Your forehead is like a piece of gold
Where a honeybee's memory hovers
Your high collar-piece of silver
Is a filigree cliff
The pleats of your multiform skirt
Randomly unfurl their waves
In the oncoming tide of dusk
Your smooth skin is like a summer breeze
From a glen strewn with pine needles
Blowing past the belly of a ewe

The dreamy swirl of your breath
On anything touched by your exhalations
Causes golden dewdrops to tremble
Your laughter is like a lark
Swooping and climbing in the sky
And it is a fact most definite
That because of your dancing feet
The collisions that raise mountains
The urges of horn to butt against horn
All foretell the ripeness of autumn

* The *agachamo* bird is praised among the Nuosu for its beauty and its elegant neck.

彝人

有人想从你的身后
去寻找那熟悉的背景
褐色的山，崎岖的路
有人想从你的身后
去寻找那种沉重的和谐
远处的羊群，低矮的云朵
然而我知道
在滚动的车轮声中
当你吮吸贫血的阳光
却陷入了
从未有过的迷惘

NUOSU

Some may look down the road you came on
Hoping to find a background they belong to
Brown mountain color, precipitous twist of road
Some may look down the road you came on
Hoping to find that weighty harmony
Far-off sheep flock, low-hugging clouds
Yet I know
Amid the sounds of turning wheels
While trying to nurse upon anemic sunlight
You are plunged into a loss of direction
Such as you have never known

孩子和猎人的背

我愿意看你的背
它在蓝蓝的空气里移动
像一块海岛一样的陆地
这是我童年阅读的一本地理
你扛着猎枪
我也扛着猎枪
看着你的背。我只想跟着你
径直往前走
寻找那个目的
你的背上有许多森林外的算术题
有的近似谜语，我和你
只相隔一段距离
猎枪是我的笔
猎物是我的纸
句号和逗号是击中猎物的枪子
可别人说的背影
很像很像你的背影
这有什么奇怪
因为我是你的儿子
无论怎样，我只想跟着你
有时像虎，有时像狼，有时什么也不像

为了寻找那个目的，有一天傍晚
你终于倒在我身旁，整个躯体
像地震后的陆地

可别人说我的背影
很像很像你的背影
其实我只想跟着你
像森林忠实于土地
我憎恨
那来自黑夜的
后人对前人的叛逆

A CHILD AND A HUNTER'S BACK

It is my wish to see your back moving
Set off against the blue sky
Like the solid ground of an island
This is the geography I studied as a child
You shouldering a rifle
And me with a rifle as well
Watching your back, only wanting to follow you
On the path straight ahead
Toward the destination you sought
On your back I read math problems from outside the forest
Some were close to riddles, and between us
A certain distance opened
The rifle was my pen
The prey was my paper
Periods were bullets to bring down my prey
Yet people say my appearance from behind
Closely resembles your appearance from behind
And this should come as no surprise
After all, I am your child
Whatever happens, I only wish to follow you
At times like a tiger, at times like a wolf, or like nothing at all

In search of that destination, one evening
You fell down beside me, and your whole body
Resembled land hit by an earthquake

Yet people say my appearance from behind
Closely resembles your appearance from behind
Truly, I only wish to follow you
Like a forest keeping faith with the land
I can only detest it
A scion's betrayal of his forebears
Due to benightedness of the soul

孩子与森林

（你属于森林
有一天却离开了森林）
在平原的尽头
外婆那家小小房屋
成了你新的天地
青蛙和老虎的故事
是你最爱听的
在房后那群蛐蛐儿的叫声中
你又长了一岁
时间的乳齿
在你金色的耳环上消失
洁白的石灰墙上，涂满了你
绿色的思念，记忆的遥远
那是小鸟和猎狗的模样
那是小溪无声的歌唱
你在画这些画时
我知道：孩子啊我的孩子
照耀你的是森林树梢上
那轮圆圆的月亮
我知道：孩子，为了你的构思
你在梦中曾和小星星商量
要不你那双小小的小小的手
怎么会把这些童话
画得这样的这样的漂亮
孩子啊我的孩子
去年秋天的傍晚
你走得那么匆忙
为了平原去玩耍
和妈妈告别时，你竟忘了唱
森林里那支古老的民谣
那时妈妈真的生气了，在你和
外婆没有看见的地方
（因为这支歌
你平时最爱唱
它是妈妈对着月亮教你的）

孩子啊我的孩子
今天妈妈来看你
你却唱起了那支古老的民谣
（朋友，让我回去吧

THE CHILD AND THE FOREST

(You belong to the forest
Yet one day you left it)
Your grandmother's little cottage
At the edge of the plain
Became your new world
What you listened to most happily
Were stories of tigers and frogs
You grew a year older
Amid the chirps of backyard crickets
The milk teeth of time
Were ushered away
By that golden ring in your earlobe
The clean plaster walls were daubed over
With your green musings, your reclaimed memories
In the form of birds and hunting dogs
And little brooks singing wordlessly
O, child, my child, I know
The full moon shone on you
Through the tops of forest trees
While you were drawing those pictures
O, my child, I know
You probably had dream talks with little stars
How else could your small hands
Have painted those fairy tales
With such wonderful beauty?
O, child, my child
One day at dusk last autumn
You went off in such a hurry
To amuse yourself on the flatland
You forgot to sing that old forest song
When you parted from your mother
So she bottled her anger and went off
Where you and Grandma could not see
(this was the song
you liked to sing most of all
which she taught you under the moon)

O, child, my child
Today your mother comes to see you
Unexpectedly you sing that old folk song
(Friend, let me go back

我怀念我的故乡
我的妈妈呀
在那望不到边的森林里
我的模样很像她的模样）
于是你要跟着妈妈走
孩子啊我的孩子
爸爸还等在家乡森林的小路上

I miss my native place
I think of my mother, far off in the forest
That stretches as far as the eye can see
And how much I resemble her)
And you wish so much to leave with her
O, child, my child
Your father awaits you along a forest lane
In your native place

最后的传说

猎人离开人世的时候，
他会听见大山的呼唤。

——引自猎人的话

死亡像一只狼
狼的皮毛是灰色的
它跑到我的木门前
对着我嗥叫
时间一定是不早了
只好对着熟睡的孙子
作一次快慰的微笑
然后我
走向呼唤我的大山
爬一座高高的乳房
当子夜时分叩响
潮湿的安魂曲
我在森林世界的
母腹里睡去
耳朵里灌满了泉水的声音
嘴唇上沾满了母亲的乳汁
天亮了
人们只听见森林里
有一个婴儿的歌声
猎人们都去把他寻找
可谁也没把他找到
于是这个神秘的故事
便成一篇关于我的童话
猎人的孩子们
都会背诵它

THE FINAL LEGEND

> When a hunter leaves this world, he hears the call of the great mountains.
>
> —The words of a hunter

Death is like a wolf
A wolf with gray fur
That runs up to my wooden door
And howls for me
The hour is surely not early
I can only give a comforting smile
To my grandson, who is fast asleep
Then I set out walking
Toward the great mountain that calls me
And climb onto its towering breast
When midnight strikes the notes
Of a damp requiem
I sleep in the womb
Of that forest realm
With the splash of spring water
Pouring in my ears
My lips moist with mother's milk
When dawn comes, people hear nothing
But a baby singing in the forest
Hunters go to look for him
But cannot find him
Soon this mysterious incident
Becomes a tale about me
The children of hunters
Can all retell it

思念

我读你的信
读秋后森林里一片黄金般的树叶
九月是玫瑰色的
树叶张着嘴
吻着热恋的土地
当树叶被温柔的风托起
悄然离开了你
却向我飘去
那时请相信，亲爱的
在我拾到它后的那片刻
我才真正读懂了
你用猎枪和男子汉的勇气
写出的，森林里一首长诗的经历

我们在黎明时别离
一只太阳鸟，将从你
云一样的背后升起
那时我会一千遍地去看
它斑斓的羽翼
这上面新长出了
好些关于你和森林的故事
它还用甜甜的高音
在碧蓝碧蓝的天宇上
撒满了星星一样密的诗句
我知道，那是要我
读黄昏从遥远处走来
读炊烟在细雨中散开
读你的沉默和篝火旁的胸腔
它呼吸像大海

我读你的信
有时甚至会读到熊的脚印
在树叶和树叶之间，布满了许多
难以预测的
兽对人的攻击
这时我总要把这封信
装进少女丰满的怀里
只愿它离我的心脏更近
于是一个长长的长长的白昼
将在我的盼望中过去

IN MIND

I have read your letter about the autumn forest
How the brilliant leaves in September
Take on a hue of roses
How leaves curve like open mouths
To kiss the land they love
One leaf was lifted by warm wind
To drift away from you
And quietly reach me
Believe me, dear
When I bent to retrieve it and read it
I finally understood what you had been through
Writing a long poem of the forest
With rifle in hand and manly courage

When we part at dawn
A sunbird will rise
Like a cloud behind your back
A thousand times my eyes will turn
Toward its speckled wing feathers
And the stories of you and the forest
That are taking a new form there
The bird will sing sweet tenor notes
In the azure vault of sky
As it strews poetic lines as thick as stars
I know they will be written to let me
Read the approach of twilight from afar
Read of cooking smoke fading in rain
And your silence beside a campfire
And your chest that heaves like an ocean

I have read your letter
In places I even read a bear's footprints
Between leaf and leaf, there were many signs
Of unpredictable attacks
Of beast against man
At such times I placed the letter
Against the swell of my youthful breasts
Only wanting it closer to my heart
Thus the long daylight hours unroll
In the midst of my anticipation

当黑夜真的来临
我们便在那棵偷听情话的
菩提树下
悄悄相会

When dark night at last approaches
Beneath the bodhi tree
That listens to secrets
We will meet

獐哨

吹母獐的声音，
公獐将向着我走来，
死亡就在这个时候降临了。

—— 一个猎人的话

我用全部的勇气吹响獐哨
吹出母獐的声音
我的肺是浓缩的海洋
一个鼻管是长江
还有一个鼻管是黄河
哨音起伏像黄昏时的波浪
掀起好些看不见的
属于母性的阳光
气体是金黄色金黄色的
悄然浮动，那么长长的绵绵的
这样温情纤细的诗行
它好像神秘地嫁给了
那柔软的光
要不就穿上了一件
雄性能用皮肤
去感觉的
如水的衣裳
但我永远明白
我是一个男性的吹哨人
每一片树叶都在为我降落伪装
我像一次误了时的约会那样等待
连焦急也变得神圣
猎枪却默默地长长地伸着
瞄向那只迟迟赶来的公獐
让它走在欺骗的身旁
于是我扣动扳机
公獐迎接了最后的死亡

当我的哨声和枪声消失了
片刻过后我好像又看见许多
母性的阳光
把一个世界照耀得那么的辉煌
不知为什么，我心里骤然掠过
一股深秋的风
像北极的冬天那么悲凉
我把獐哨咬破了

DEER WHISTLE

> Blow a doe's cry until the buck draws near; that is when death will descend upon him.
>
> —The words of a hunter

With all my courage, I blow the deer whistle
Blow the cry of a mother deer
An ocean is condensed in my lungs
Twin rivers run through my nostrils
The whistle notes quaver like waves at twilight
They stir all the sunbeams
With invisible feminine excitation
Elusive in the warm-toned golden air
Floating in a tender, drawn-out thread
Such a long and slender line of verse
It seems mysteriously married
To the soft light
Or perhaps it has put on
A suit of watery clothes
Which can best be felt
By a male deer's skin
But it is always clear to me
I am a man blowing the whistle
Each leaf falls to give me camouflage
Like an unkept rendezvous I wait
My anxious mood turns solemn
As my mute rifle stays raised and ready
Aiming at the buck that haltingly draws near
Letting him approach the proximity of deception
And then I pull the trigger
And the buck meets his death

When the whistle sound and gunshot fade away
At that moment I seem to see
A feminine cast in the sunbeams
Transfixing the world with such radiance
I know not why a gust of autumn wind
Would pass over my heart
Bringing a sad arctic chill
I split the whistle with my teeth

连同嘴唇上的血
甩在了谁也看不见的地方

说实话
那时我有些想哭
还想撒谎
我怕那些爱我的人们知道

And throw it, along with blood from my lip
Into a place no one can see

Truthfully speaking
I was close to crying then
I wanted to tell a lie
Fearing that my loved ones would know

英雄结和猎人

头颅上圆圆的建筑
布裹成了尖端
盘山的路在这里结尾
绕山的河在这里流完
对着天空湛蓝的海洋
伸着一根长长的鱼竿

鱼竿在蓝蓝的空气里
牵动着白云和白云一样的炊烟
在黎明的微光中
那是一张有着高鼻梁的剪纸
他哼出的每一口气和雾
都在森林中悄悄地跑了
只有到黄昏才能看见
他和猎狗褐色的影子
这样走着，真是太神气了
嘴里还衔着又酸又涩的野果
目光是又长又短的钓线
颜色是金黄金黄的
全怪篝火和麂子肉的熏染
它在眼前寻觅熊的脚迹
钓竿晃悠悠地在呼喊
使得小松鼠蹦跳得遥远遥远
然后他在斜坡上歇息
让大黑狗在身旁坐着伸长舌头
舔着黄昏滴下的米酒
而钓竿照样直直地伸着

THE HERO'S KNOT AND THE HUNTER*

The round-tipped structure rising from the skull
Where a wrapping of cloth reaches its apex
Brings a spiral mountain road to its end
A curving mountain stream flows to its limit
Into the pellucid ocean of sky
It extends its long fishing rod

Amid blue air, this fishing rod
Tugs at clouds and cloudy cooking smoke
Each puff of mist exhaled
In the faint light of dawn
By this aquiline cutout
Dissolves away into the forest
Only in slanting sunlight can you see
Two earthly shadows, cast by the knot and a hound
The knot has a pompous way of moving
While in its puckered mouth it carries a seed
Its fishing-line gaze spools long and short
Its color is a burnished brown
Which can be blamed on wood smoke and venison
Before its eyes there are bear tracks to be examined
The fishing rod swings in a beckoning manner
Causing little squirrels to scamper away
And then the hunter rests on the slope of a hill
Letting his black dog sit and loll its tongue
To lap up rice wine that drizzles down at dusk
But the fishing rod stands as straight as ever

* A "hero's knot" is a decorative appendage on the traditional male headdress of the Nuosu. Made of tightly wrapped cloth with a round bulge at the tip, it extends upward and forward from the crown of the head.

森林，猎人的蜜蜡珠

风像一群顽皮的姑娘
折四季的山野剪纸
把你双耳的形状
剪在森林蓝色记忆的海上
从此白桦林一个劲地长
从此青㭎林一个劲地长
从此你神奇的双耳
便成了两只张开翅膀的小鸟
猎人，你的耳朵能长翅膀
你的耳朵是孕育的树
在森林的北方一个劲地长
在森林的南方一个劲地长
长给你的父亲看
长给你的母亲看
那个洋洋自得的太阳
那个羞羞答答的月亮
于是你的耳中那很薄很薄的耳膜
便穿上了雾的衣裳
于是你耳中阡阡陌陌的毛细血管
便成了数不清的溪流
应着饮水的野鸡歌唱

你听到秋天在树叶上散步
那儿集合星星一样的船队
船长在摆动三叶草起锚
那儿飘满了蜻蜓的乐曲
雪白的蝴蝶披着彩虹的晨曦
那儿昆虫在甜言蜜语

你听到松鼠在隐藏诗句
那是太阳鸟写给黎明的序
可蚂蚁却在偷听别人的秘密
你听见獐子背着七月的森林
躯体上发出金属的声音
岩羊在那个潮湿的地方
制造一次无名的美丽
你听见了森林中一切的一切
都在那里展示赤裸的活力
都在那里预言爱情的风暴

猎人，猎人，我们的猎人

THE FOREST AND A HUNTER'S WAX BEAD

Each season the wind, like a bevy of playful girls
Folds a cutout of mountain wilderness
And snips out the shapes of your ears
Against a blue sea of forest memories
Whereupon a birch grove grows eagerly
Whereupon a maple grove grows eagerly
Whereupon your marvelous ears
Turn into birds on the wing
Hunter, your ears can grow wings
Your ears are pregnant with a sapling
Growing eagerly north of the forest
Growing eagerly south of the forest
Growing for your father to see
Growing for your mother to see
For the lordly, self-assured sun
For the demure and bashful moon
Whereupon your eardrum, so sheer and thin
Puts on a robe of mist
While tiny vessels in your ear, like the borders of fields
Turn into countless streams that sing
In answer to chickens at a watering place

You listen to autumn ambling through tree leaves
A star-like convoy has assembled there
A captain steering a clover leaf weighs anchor
The air is adrift with dragonfly melodies
In a spot where insects exchange confidences
A snowy butterfly wears a cape of rosy dawn

You hear squirrels hiding caches of poetic lines
For use in a prelude the sunbird will write for dawn
While ants eavesdrop on people's secrets
You hear water deer reciting the July forest
Each of their bodies gives off a clarion call
And mountain goats in drizzling mists
Are crafting a nameless beauty
You hear every single thing in the forest
How it manifests life's urge nakedly
How it foretells a storm of love

Hunter, O hunter, I see the forest

森林是蓝色的蜜蜡珠
被你戴在男性的耳垂上
让宇宙女神浴着银河欣赏
照耀你的是永恒的太阳

In the blue bead of beeswax
That you wear on your manly earlobe
To regale the goddess who bathes in the Milky Way
Watching you illumined by the eternal sun

泸沽湖

有人说泸沽湖是山姑娘，狮子山是她的母亲。
奇怪的是这位母亲，永远不让自己的女儿出嫁。

——题记

蓝色的裙裾在朦胧的雾中失落了
哦，山姑娘你在哪里？
去问狮子吧。她是山姑娘永恒的母亲
一个固执得像石头一样的女人
一个由于冷酷过早衰老的寡妇

好多年了，她把山姑娘紧紧地搂在怀中
连风也不知道这是长眠着的一个人
一个不是少女的处女
一个贞洁得不该贞洁的女人
风。那充满野性的风
这是男子痴情的语言，他曾在岸边徘徊
但这一切早已过去了，像一个遥远的梦
心。无数男人的心，都沉入了一片死寂的海
变态的母亲，一个无辜少女的坟墓
山姑娘真可怜，她还沉睡着，睡得是那样安然
她裸露着全身，在自己的梦中
在那绸缎般起伏的床上哭泣。难道她只会这样？
千万年了，母亲成了石头，少女的心化成了水
男人呢？
失恋的打鱼人

LUGU LAKE

> Some people say that Lugu Lake is a highland maiden and Lion Mountain is her mother. For some strange reason, this mother would not let her daughter be married off.

The blue gown is lost in obscuring mist
Where are you, young lady of the mountains?
Go ask the lioness, eternal mother of the highland maiden
A woman as obstinate as rock
A heartless widow, old before her time

For so many years she held the highland girl in her embrace
Even the wind forgets this is a spellbound woman
An old maid whose chastity was not right for her
This wild wind was the lovestruck speech
Of a youth who used to pace the shore
But all of this has passed like a distant dream
Of the heart. Countless men's hearts sank into this still lake
An abnormal mother, the grave of a guiltless girl
Pity the highland maiden, still fast asleep, sleeping with such poise
Her whole body is exposed as she dreams away
Weeping on her bed that ripples like brocade
Is this all she will ever know?
Thousands of years have passed, the mother has turned to stone
The girl's heart has turned to water
As for the man?
A lovelorn fisherman

朵洛荷舞

是因为荒野太宽了
她们才牵着彼此的手
踩着神经一样敏感的舞步
要不然，那土地上的
软绵绵的，紫云英的梦
就会踩破，就会踩破
留给黄昏几瓣孤寂的花朵

流吧，淌出的是一条旋转的河
唱吧，哼出的是一支古老的歌

于是黑夜来临之前
便有着高傲的心，便有着痴情的眼
还有了疲倦的口弦
可她们的舞步照样走着，照样呢喃
对着土地，对着黎明，对着遥远
一脚踩着一个打湿了的，淡绿色的梦幻
一脚踩着一个温柔的，溢满了蜜的呼唤
这一声，那么缠绵，那么缠绵

THE *DULOHXO* DANCE*

Is it because the wilderness is so vast
That they take each other by the hand
Treading with steps as delicate as nerve ends
Lest the dream upon that land
That tenderly played-out milk-vetch dream
Be interrupted by their footfalls
Leaving a few lonely petals in the dusk

So flow on, to issue in swirling dreams
Sing on, giving voice to ancient melody

And so before the dark night falls
Here are things to swell a prideful heart
To captivate the eye
And drive a mouth harp to exhaustion
But still the dance steps go on, incantations continue
Addressed to the land, to dawn and faraway things
One foot taps out a wet, succulent dream
One foot taps out a tender, honeyed summons
So enticing is this sound, so very enticing

---

* The *dulohxo* dance is performed by dancers who join hands in a ring and turn about slowly.

唱给母亲的歌

凉山上有不少高山湖，过去多有一对对雁鹅栖息。每年雁行经过时，大雁都要把子雁送入雁行。子雁不想离开，大雁便用翅膀拍打子雁，逼其加入雁行，飞去飞回往返多次才能送走。这一天，附近的群众都要赶来观看，妇女无不流泪。

——题记

只因为北方没有了雪
只因为一次
最遥远的旅行
从这里开始
当子雁的叫声传来
啊，母亲
我真的不敢
大声地出气
我真的不敢啊
睁开眼睛

就这样过了很久很久
我才悄悄朝远方望去
天上再没有子雁的影子
地上再没有子雁的声音
啊，母亲
这时你哭了
紧搂着我
不停地抽泣

只因为他乡也有星星
只因为女人
到了出嫁的年龄
就要远去
不知是什么时候
当我骑着披红的马走向远山
我回过头来看见
夕阳早已剪断了
通往故乡的小路

A SONG FOR MOTHER

> In the Liangshan mountains, there are many lakes where pairs of wild geese used to live. Each year when migratory flocks passed overhead, the local wild geese would send their young off to join the migration. The young geese were reluctant to leave, so the parents had to force them, using flat blows of their wings, to join the passing flocks. It took several back-and-forth flights before the parents could finally get their young to leave. On days when this happened, people who lived nearby would rush to see the spectacle, and women in the crowd would always weep.

Because there was no more snow in the north
Because it was time
for a distant journey
to begin from here
When the goslings' voices resounded
O, Mother
I truly could not bear
to take a loud breath
I truly could not bear
to open my eyes wide

After a long while
I furtively raised my head to look
No young geese could be seen in the sky
No young geese could be heard on the shore
O, Mother
That moment you were crying
hugging me tightly
sobbing on and on

Because stars also shine in other places
Because a girl
who reaches a certain age
has to go far away
I cannot say which day I set out for distant mountains
Riding a horse decked out in red
I turned my head and saw
the path to my hometown
was cut off by the sunset

啊，母亲
这时我看见你
独自站在那高高的山岗上
用你多皱的双手
捧着苍老的脸
——哭泣
啊，母亲
只有在今天
我才真正懂得了
为了那子雁的离去
你为什么
曾经那样伤心
啊，母亲
我最亲爱的母亲

O, Mother
That moment I saw you
Standing all alone
On a high hill
Covering your timeworn face
with wrinkled fingers—sobbing
O, Mother
The day has come
that I truly understand
Why the departure of geese
once filled you
with such sadness
Why you grieved so
O, Mother
my dear, beloved mother

史诗和人

我仿佛感到山在遥远处隐去
我仿佛感到海在我身边安息
我仿佛感到土地在无止境地延伸
我仿佛感到天空布满了蓝黑色的旋律
我仿佛感到爱像黄昏的小雨
我仿佛感到在一支民族迁徙的路上
那些牛的脚印
那些羊的脚印
那些男人的脚印
那些女人的脚印
都变成了永恒

我好像看见祖先的天菩萨被星星点燃
我好像看见祖先的肌肉是群山的造型
我好像看见祖先的躯体上长出了荞子
我好像看见金黄的太阳变成了一盏灯
我好像看见土地上有一部古老的日记
我好像看见山野里站立着一群沉思者
最后我看见一扇门上有四个字
《勒俄特依》
于是我敲开了这扇沉重的门
这时我看见远古洪荒的地平线上
飞来一只鹰
这时我看见未来文明的黄金树下
站着一个人

THE EPIC AND THE MAN

I feel as if mountains are hidden in the distance
I feel as if an ocean rests beside me
I feel that the land extends without end
I feel love like a shower at twilight
I feel that the night-blue sky is filled with melodies
I feel that along the route of a people's migration
All the hoofprints of oxen
The hoofprints of sheep
The footprints of men and women
Have been immortalized

I seem to see the ancestors' sky god lit in starlight
I seem to see the ancestors' muscles in the curves of distant
    mountains
I seem to see buckwheat growing from the ancestors' bodies
I seem to see the golden sun turned into a lamp
I seem to see an ancient diary on the land
I seem to see a group of deep thinkers standing in the highlands
I seem to see a door bearing the words *Book of Origins**
Whereupon I push that heavy door open
On the horizon of antiquity I see an eagle flying toward me
And then under the golden tree of a future civilization
I see a human being standing

* *Hne-wo Te-yy* (or *Hnex-wop Tep-yy*) is a Nuosu epic, known in English as the *Book of Origins*.

达基沙洛故乡

我承认一切痛苦来自那里
我承认一切悲哀来自那里
我承认不幸的传说也显得神秘
我承认所有的夜晚都充满了忧郁
我承认血腥的械斗就发生在那里
我承认我十二岁的叔叔曾被亲人送去抵命
我承认单调的日子
我承认那些过去的岁月留下的阴影
我承认夏夜的星空在瓦板屋顶是格外的迷人
我承认诞生
我承认死亡
我承认光着身子的孩子爬满了土墙
我承认那些平常的生活
我承认母亲的笑意里也含着惆怅
啊，我承认这就是生我养我的故土
纵然有一天我到了富丽堂皇的石姆姆哈
我也要哭喊着回到她的怀中

DEJYSHALO, MY NATIVE PLACE

I admit that all pain comes from there
I admit that all sorrow comes from there
I admit that its tales of trouble have an air of mystery
I admit that the nights are all filled with melancholy
I admit that bloody feuds happened there
I admit that my twelve-year-old uncle was given in forfeit for a life
I admit the monotonous days
I admit the shadows left by passing years
I admit the summer enchantment of stars over a tile roof
I admit the births, I admit the deaths
I admit naked children crawling all over an earthen wall
I admit the everyday routines
I admit a disconsolate note in my mother's laugh
Ah, I admit this was the homeland that birthed and nurtured me
Even if I go someday to elysian Shymumuhxa*
I will sob to return to her embrace

* Shymumuhxa is a peaceful limbo-like realm between heaven and earth where souls go after death.

等待

——一个彝女的呓语

从火塘边到石磨旁
白天对于我们来说，很快
就要消失掉。然后
是爬上木梯，然后
是蜷曲着身体睡觉
每天是这样
每月是这样
就是半夜醒来，看见
月亮和星星也迷惘

即使我们到山下的
街上去，买回一个圆镜
它也照不见远处的风景
最好是坐在木门前
拿一根针穿透梦，有时
也会把手刺伤，但是
这决不会打扰忧郁的歌唱
数不清这是多少个日子
天亮时总要听见公鸡叫
只要一看见那红黄黑的衣裳
谁都要说：绣得真漂亮！
啊，明日就是火把节了
在温暖的草堆里，影子听见
我疲惫的骨节开始发响

WAITING

—Dream-babble of a Nuosu woman

Between the fireplace and the millstone
The daylight hours slip away
Before we know it, and then
We climb a wooden ladder, and then
We curl our bodies and sleep
Every day is like this
Every month is like this
Even while lying awake, we feel lost
Watching the moon and stars

Even when we go down the mountain
Onto a street and buy ourselves a mirror
It reflects no distant scenes
It is best to sit before the wooden door
Take a needle and pass it through a dream
Sometimes we prick our hands, but this
Never breaks off our moody song

Who can keep track of how many days
I have listened for the rooster's cry at dawn
But whoever sees this red, black, and yellow dress
Will say the needlework is fine!
Ah, tomorrow is the Torch Festival
Shadows in the warm straw pile know
My weary bones have begun to creak

火神

自由在火光中舞蹈。信仰在火光中跳跃
死亡埋伏着黑暗，深渊睡在身边
透过洪荒的底片，火是猎手的衣裳
抛弃寒冷那个素雅的女性，每一句
咒语，都像光那样自豪，罪恶在开花
颤栗的是土地，高举着变了形的太阳
把警告和死亡，送到苦难生灵的梦魂里
让恐慌飞跑，要万物在静谧中吉祥
猛兽和凶神，在炽热的空间里消亡
用桃形的心打开白昼，黎明就要难产
一切开始。不是鸡叫那一声，是我睁眼那一霎

GOD OF FIRE

Freedom dances in the blaze, faith leaps in the blaze
Death lurks in darkness, the abyss sleeps by my side
From the developing bath of primal chaos, fire will clothe the
  hunter
So cast off coldness—that prim female—make each chanted verse
As prideful as light, for flowers of sin are blooming
Setting the land atremble as it raises a deformed sun
Sending alarm and death into the dreams of suffering souls
Let panic flee, if beings are to be blessed with tranquility
Let beasts and demons be consumed in the blazing space
With a peach-shaped heart, usher in daylight, dawn will have its
  labor pains
It all begins, not at the cock's crow, but the instant I open my eyes

老歌手

唱完一支少女时的歌
你害羞了, 脸上泛起红晕
就是那双苍老的眼
骤然间仿佛也跳出了两颗迷人的星
沿着你满脸皱纹的沟壑
你蹒跚着走进了自己的记忆
啊, 这是一块被风雨耕耘过的土地
在那褐色土地的边缘
你珍藏着一个女人最宝贵的东西——
它是你白天的太阳
它是你晚上的月亮
在你的瞳孔里升起一道彩虹
但这是湖边虚幻的彩虹
那时白天和黑夜的梦都属于你
那时男人们都在梦中离开了你
黎明时, 他们走了
带走的是你的容貌, 留下的是你的心
为了把他们等待
你至今还唱着那时的歌

OLD SONGSTRESS

After singing the song you learned in girlhood
You feel shy, your face blushes scarlet
And two enchanting stars seem ready to jump
Out from your careworn eyes
You totter back into your memory
Along the gullies of your wrinkled face
Ah, this land is harrowed by wind and rain
At the margin of this brown land
You cherish a woman's most precious thing—
It is the sun of your daytime
It is the moon of your evening
It raises a rainbow in your sight
But only a dreamy rainbow by a lake
Dream-filled days and nights were yours back then
But all the men left you in a dream back then
By the light of dawn they went away
Taking the bloom of your youth, leaving behind your heart
Even today you sing that song
It marks your hours of waiting for them

狮子山上的禅寺

——写给僧人建文皇帝

一个昔日的君主
微闭着眼
盘腿坐在黑暗的深处
油灯淡黄的光影
禅寺中虚空的气息
把他的袈裟变得不再真实
他偶有睁眼的时候
那是一个年迈的僧人
正蹒跚着跨过那道
越来越高的门槛
他知道这个人是监察御史叶希贤
一位跟随他流亡多年的大臣
唉，现在他们都老了
只能生活在缥缈的回忆里
难怪就在他踏入暗影的一瞬间
君王的眼里，掠过了一丝笑意
此时他想到了权力以及至尊的地位
在死亡和时间的面前是这般脆弱
已经很长时间了，他什么都不再相信
因为他看见过青春的影子
如何在岁月的河流中消失

THE BUDDHIST MONASTERY ON LION MOUNTAIN

—For the Buddhist monk who was formerly Emperor Jianwen*

A man who was formerly a ruler
Sits cross-legged in darkness
With eyelids lowered
Faint beams cast by an oil lamp
And the stillness of the meditation hall
Give his cassock a touch of unreality
Now and then his eyes open
To see an aged monk
Walk across the high threshold
With an unsteady step
He knows it is Ye Xixian, his former councilor
The high official who shares his long exile
Ah, they have grown old now
No life is left them but dreamy memories
No wonder a smile crinkles the ruler's eyes
Watching his friend enter the shadows
He realizes that power and exalted rank
Are all too helpless against death and time
Years ago, he gave up believing in anything
For he had seen youthful shapes
Fade away in the river of years

* Emperor Jianwen of the Ming Dynasty reigned from 1399 to 1403, when he was removed from power by his uncle Zhu Di, who became Emperor Cheng. According to folk tradition, the deposed emperor became a monk at a temple in Yunnan.

酒的怀念

怀念酒
就是怀念一段久远的历史
怀念酒
就是怀念一个老去的山村
怀念酒
你会想起一个多年不见的朋友
怀念酒
你会想起一本久违了的旧书
怀念酒
有时就如同听一支老歌
泪水会不知不觉从眼眶里流出
怀念酒
仿佛自己又回到一条时间的雨巷
那些我们曾经历过的所有的欢乐和痛苦
将会在一个瞬间又回到记忆的门槛

THINKING OF WINE

Thinking of wine
Is reliving a long-ago chapter of history
Thinking of wine
Is thinking back to an old mountain village
Thinking of wine
You recall a friend not seen for years
Thinking of wine
You recall a long-unread book
Thinking of wine
Is like hearing a snatch of old song
Tears brim in your eyes before you know it
Thinking of wine
Is like walking down the rainy alleyway of time
All those joys and pains we went through
Return in an instant to memory's threshold

土墙

——我原来一直不知道，以色列的石头，能让犹太人感动。

远远望过去
土墙在阳光下像一种睡眠

不知为什么
在我的意识深处
常常幻化出的
都是彝人的土墙

我一直想破译
这其中的秘密
因为当我看见那道墙时
我的伤感便会油然而生

其实墙上什么也没有

EARTHEN WALL

—For a long time I did not know that stones in Israel could move a Jewish person

Looked at from a distance
The earthen wall in sunlight seems to be asleep

I wonder why
Deep in my consciousness
The image that often appears
Is this earthen wall of the Nuosu

I always try to decipher
The secret behind this
Because when I see that wall
Sadness wells up in my heart

In truth, nothing is there but a wall

献给土著民族的颂歌

——为联合国世界土著人年而写

歌颂你
就是歌颂土地
就是歌颂土地上的河流
以及那些数不清的属于人类的居所

理解你
就是理解生命
就是理解生殖和繁衍的缘由
谁知道有多少不知名的种族
曾在这个大地上生活

怜悯你
就是怜悯我们自己
就是怜悯我们共同的痛苦和悲伤
有人看见我们骑着马
最后消失在所谓文明的城市中

抚摸你
就是抚摸人类的良心
就是抚摸人类美好和罪恶的天平
多少个世纪以来，历史已经证明
土著民族所遭受的迫害是最为残暴的

祝福你
就是祝福玉米，祝福荞麦，祝福土豆
就是祝福那些世界上最古老的粮食
为此我们没有理由不把母亲所给予的生命和梦想
毫无保留地献给人类的和平、自由与公正

A PRAISE SONG FOR INDIGENOUS PEOPLES

—Written for the United Nations Year of Indigenous Peoples

To sing in praise of you
Is to sing in praise of the land
It is to praise the rivers on the land
And the countless human habitats

To understand you
Is to understand the will to live
It is to understand how people can be fruitful and multiply
Who knows how many races, now nameless
Once lived upon this good earth?

To pity you
Is to pity ourselves
It is to pity our shared pain and sorrow
A certain man watched us riding on horseback
Until we vanished into a so-called civilized city

To caress you
Is to caress the human conscience
It is to caress the scales that weigh human decency and evil
Over so many centuries, history has proven
Indigenous peoples have suffered the cruelest harm

To bless you
Is to bless corn and buckwheat and potatoes
It is to bless this world's most ancient foodstuffs
Thus it would only be right to give, without reservation
The life and dreams our mother gave us
As an offering for peace, freedom, and human justice

欧姬芙的家园

——献给二十世纪最伟大的美国女画家

或许这是最寂寞的家园
离开尘世是那样的遥远
风吹过荒原的低处，告诉我们
只有一个人在这里等待

这是离上帝最近的高地
否则就不会听见
那天籁般的声音最终变成色彩
从容地穿过那纯洁的世界

你的手是神奇的语言
牛骨和石头被装饰成一道黑门
谁知道在你临终的时候
曼陀罗的叹息是如此沉重

欧姬芙，一个梦的化身
你的虚无和神秘都是至高无上的
因为现实的存在，从来就没有证明过
一个女人生命的全部！

O'KEEFFE'S HOMELAND

—To America's greatest female painter of the twentieth century

Perhaps this is the loneliest homeland
Being so very far from mundane things
Wind blowing across wasteland hollows tells us
Only one person could be waiting here

This high country is closest to God
Or else you would never have heard
Those heavenly panpipes that turned to colors
As they passed unimpeded through this pure realm

Your hands held a marvelous language
That opened a dark gate in stone and skull ornaments
Who would think, when your hour of passing came
The mandrake root would sigh so heavily?

O'Keeffe, you were a dream made flesh
Your emptiness and mystery were the most exalted
Never had existing reality offered such evidence
Of everything a woman's life could be

回望二十世纪

——献给纳尔逊·曼德拉

站在时间的岸边
站在一个属于精神的高地
我在回望二十世纪
此时我没有眼泪
欢乐和痛苦都变得陌生
我好像站在另一个空间
在审视人类一段奇特的历史

其实这一百年
战争与和平从未离开过我们
而对暴力的控诉也未曾停止
有人歌唱过自由
也有人献身于民主
但人类经历得最多的还是专制和迫害
其实这一百年
诞生过无数伟大的幻想
但灾难却也接踵而至
其实这一百年
多种族的人类，把文明又一次推向了顶峰
我们都曾在地球的某一个角落
悄悄地流下过感激的泪水
二十世纪
你让一部分人欢呼和平的时候
却让另一部分人的两眼布满仇恨的影子
你让黑人在大街上祈求人权
却让残杀和暴力出现在他们家中
你让我们认识卡尔·马克思的同时
也让我们见到了尼采
你让我们看见爱因斯坦是怎样提出了相对论
你同时又让我们目睹这个人最后成为基督徒
你曾把许多巨人的思想变得虚无
你也曾把某个无名者的话语铅印成真理
你散布过阿道夫·希特勒的法西斯主张
你宣扬过圣雄甘地的非暴力主义
你让社会主义在一些国家获得成功
同时你又让国际工人运动处于了低潮
在诞生弗洛伊德的泛性论年代

LOOKING BACK ON THE TWENTIETH CENTURY

—For Nelson Mandela

Standing on the riverbank of time
Standing on a vantage point belonging to spirit
I look back upon the twentieth century
Just now I have no tears
Joy and agony have grown alien to me
I seem to stand in an alternate space
As I scan an amazing segment of human history

For a fact, in these hundred years
War and peace were never far from us
And denunciations of violence never ceased
Some people sang of freedom
Some offered themselves up for democracy
But tyranny and mistreatment were the lot of all too many
For a fact, in these hundred years
Countless memorable fantasies took birth
Yet disasters followed on their heels
For a fact, in these hundred years
Multiracial humanity reached a new peak of civilization
For which we have all wept tears of gratitude
In our respective corners of the globe
O twentieth century
You let some people cheer for peace
But darkened the eyes of others with hatred
You sent black people onto the streets, calling for human rights
Then you allowed slaughter and violence to erupt in their homelands
You let us make the acquaintance of Karl Marx
You also let us meet Friedrich Nietzsche
You let us see Einstein propose the theory of relativity
Then let us watch him become a Christian in the end
You reduced the thoughts of giants to emptiness
While printing the pronouncements of a nobody as truth
You spread the fascist doctrines of Adolf Hitler
And you publicized the pacifism of the sage Gandhi
You allowed socialism to win success in certain countries
While letting the international workers' movement ebb away
In an age that spawned Freud's doctrine of pansexualism

你推崇过霍梅尼和伊斯兰革命
你为了马丁·路德·金闻名全世界
却让这个人以被别人枪杀为代价
你在非洲产生过博卡萨这样可以吃人肉的独裁者
同样你也在非洲养育了人类的骄子纳尔逊·曼德拉
你叫柏林墙在一夜之间倒塌
你却又叫车臣人和俄罗斯人产生仇恨
还没有等阿拉伯人和犹太人真正和解
你又在科索沃引发了新的危机和冲突
你让人类在极度纵欲的欢娱之后
最后却要承受艾滋病的痛苦和折磨
你的确让人类看到了遗传工程的好处
却又让人类的精神在工业文明的泥沼中异化而亡
你把信息时代的技术
传播到了拉丁美洲最边远的部落
你却又让一种文化在没有硝烟的地方
消灭另一种文化
你在欧洲降下人们渴望已久的冬雪
你却又在哥伦比亚暴雨如注
使一个印第安人的村庄毁灭于山洪
你让我们在月球上遥望美丽的地球
使我们相信每一个民族都是兄弟
可你又让我们因宗教而产生分歧与离异
在巴尔干和耶路撒冷相互屠杀
你让高科技移植我们需要的器官
你又让这些器官感受到核武器的恐惧
在纽约人们关心更多的是股市的涨跌
但在非洲饥饿和瘟疫却时刻威胁着人类
是的，二十世纪
当我真的回望你的时候
我才发现你是如此的神秘
你是必然，又是偶然
你仿佛证明的是过去
似乎预示着的又是未来
你好像是上帝在无意间
遗失的一把锋利无比的双刃剑

You glorified Khomeini and the Islamic revolution
You let Martin Luther King win worldwide fame
Then you made him pay for it by being gunned down
In Africa you produced the dictator Bokassa, capable of
cannibalism
Also in Africa you reared Nelson Mandela—the pride of humanity
You brought down the Berlin Wall overnight
Yet you fomented hatred between Chechnya and Russia
Without waiting for Arabs and Jews to reach true accord
You set off a new conflict and crisis in Kosovo
You let humans revel in extreme indulgence
Then subjected them to the pain and torment of AIDS
You let people see clear advances in genetic engineering
But you alienated men's spirits in an industrial morass
You developed the technology of the information age
And transferred it to the remotest tribes of Latin America
Yet you allowed one culture to erase another
Without even resorting to gunpowder
In Europe you sent much-awaited snow for skiing
But in Colombia your downpours were so heavy
That an Indian village was washed away by flash floods
You let us gaze on the lovely earth from the moon
Causing us to believe that all people are brothers
Yet you also turned us against each other with religious differences
And let massacres happen in Jerusalem and the Balkans
You brought technology that made organ transplants possible
And made those organs feel dread over nuclear weapons
In New York City, you preoccupied us with market fluctuations
While people in Africa were still threatened by disease and famine
O twentieth century
When I truly look back upon you
I discover what an enigma you are
You were necessity, but you were also randomness
You seemed to be a confirmation of the past
You also seemed to presage the future
God seems to have lost hold of you for a moment
And you fell to us, a double-edged sword

我承认，我爱这座城市

这个城市的午后
是阳光最美好的时刻
鸽群的影子，穿行在
高楼与林木的四周
那些消失的
雾霭和青烟
如同玛瑙的碎片
闪烁在远处的群山之间
这个城市的无穷魅力，或许
就是因为它的起伏不平
它的美是神秘的，像一则寓言

我承认，我爱这个城市
那是因为我每次见到它
它给我的惊喜和陌生的感觉
要远远超过我对它的熟悉
它似乎永远埋藏着一种激情
就像一个年轻而又充满了
野性的少妇
每当我看见夜色
沉落在歌乐山巅
山城的万家灯火，便开始演奏
一部穿越时空的交响乐
那些星星般闪耀的音符
集合起金色的船队
把这座东方名副其实的山城
演绎成一片波峰浪谷的
最为神奇的光的海洋
不知道为什么
往往在这样的时候
我就会想到六十多年前
这座城市所经历的
那场惨绝人寰的大轰炸
我不敢肯定，在这些灯光中
有没有死者的眼睛
在另一个世界
审视着我们
他们是因悲愤
而惊恐万分的老人

I ADMIT IT, I LOVE THIS CITY

Afternoon in this city
Is when the sunlight is most beautiful
Shadows of pigeon flocks pass
Along perimeters of groves and office towers
And those fading patches
Of valley mist and bluish haze
Gleam like pieces of veined agate
Among far-off groups of mountains
The endless allure of this city perhaps
Lies in the folds of its irregular terrain
Its beauty holds mystery, like a parable

I admit it, I love this city
Because each time I see it
I am surprised and struck by a strangeness
That far surpasses my familiarity with it
It always seems to hide a certain passion
Like a young wife
Fresh and full of wildness
Each time I watch darkness
Descend on the top of Mount Gele
The lights of this mountain city begin to perform
A symphony that leaps through time and space
Those starry twinkling notes
Assemble in a golden convoy
Recasting this mountain city of the East
As a marvelous ocean of light
Complete with wave troughs and crests
I know not why, but at such times
I think back sixty-odd years
To the bombings this city endured*
It was merciless, ultimate horror
I cannot say for sure whether eyes of the dead
Still peer out from among these lights
Examining us from another world
They belong to old people, terribly shaken
By grief and indignation

* During World War II, the Japanese army unleashed massive bombardments on Chongqing (Chunking), resulting in grave civilian casualties.

是由于窒息，流血的十指
插入防空洞土墙的妇女
是那些张着嘴，但已经死去
怀里还抱着婴儿的母亲
我知道，那是五万多生命
他们的控诉
已成为永远的呐喊

是的，我爱这座城市
还有一个特殊的原因
那就是这座伟大的城市
与它宽厚善良的人民一样
把目光永远投向未来
从不复制仇恨
在这里，时间、死亡以及生命
所铸造的全部生活
都变成了一种
能包容一切的
沉甸甸的历史记忆！
从某种意义而言
这个城市对战争的反思
对和平的渴望
就是今天的中国
对这个世界的回答！

Suffocated women whose bloody fingers
Scratched at the dirt walls of bomb shelters
They are gape-mouthed mothers, who died
With their children in their arms
I know the denunciations
Raised by those fifty thousand dead
Stand as an undying outcry

Indeed, my love for this city
Exists for another special reason
Namely that this great city
Like its kind, generous people
Always keeps its eyes on the future
Never seeking to duplicate vengeance
Here the totality of life
Compounded of time, death, and the will to live
Has been turned into historical memory
Weighty and universally tolerant!
In a sense one could say
This city's reflective attitude toward war
And its longing for peace
Are the same as what today's China
Gives as its answer to the world!

献给这个世界的河流

我承认
我曾经歌颂过你
就如同我曾经歌颂过土地和生命
在这个世界上
不知有多少诗人和智者
用不同的文字赞美过你
因为你的存在
不知又有多少诗篇
成为了人类的经典
诚然不是我第一个
把你喻为母亲
但是你的乳汁却千百年来
滋养着广袤的大地
以及在大地上生活着的人们
我承认
是你创造了最初的神话
是你用无形的手
在那金色的岸边开始了耕种
相信吧，人类所有的文明
都因为河流的养育
才充满了无限的生机
我们敬畏河流，那是因为河流是一种象征
它崇高的名字就像一部史诗
它真实地记录着人类历史的进步和苦难
我们向文明致敬
实际上就是在向那些伟大的河流致敬
是河流给了我们智慧
是河流传授给了我们不同种族的语言和文化
同样也是河流给了我们
千差万别的生活方式和信仰
我承认，河流！你的美丽曾经无与伦比
就像一个睡眠中的少女
当你走过梦幻般的田野
其实你已经把诗歌和爱情都给了我们
相信吧，在多少民族的心目中
你就是正义和自由的化身
你就是人类的良心和眼泪
你帮助过弱者，你给被压迫者以同情
你的每一罐圣水，沐浴的是人的灵魂
你给不幸的人们

DEDICATED TO THE RIVERS OF THIS WORLD

I avow
I have sung in praise of you
As I have sung in praise of the land and living things
I know not how many poets and wise men
In this world
Have praised you, each in his own script
I know not how many poems
Have entered humanity's canon
Because of your existence
Truthfully I am not the first
To liken you to a mother
But your milk still nurtures the broad land
And all the people living on it
As it did thousands of years ago
I avow
It was you who created the earliest myths
And with your invisible hands
Began tilling soil along the golden banks
Believe it, all of human civilization
Has been filled with a boundless life force
Only because of nurturing rivers
We hold rivers in awe, because rivers are a symbol
A river's honored name is like an epic
A truthful record of human progress and calamity
When we salute civilization
We are really saluting those great rivers
Our wisdom was given us by rivers
Rivers carried language and culture from other races
Likewise it was rivers that gave us
Variety of beliefs and ways of life
I avow, rivers, that your loveliness is beyond compare
Like a sleeping maiden
As you pass through dreamy fields
In truth you have given us poetry and love
Believe it, in the hearts of a host of peoples
You are the embodiment of justice and freedom
You are the conscience and the tears of humankind
You help the weak, you give sympathy to the oppressed
Each jug of your sacred water is an ablution for people's souls
To suffering people you forever grant

馈赠的永远是生活的信心和勇气
我承认，人类对你的伤害是深重的

当我们望着断流的河岸
以及你那遭到污染的身躯
我们的忏悔充满着悲伤
相信吧，河流！我们向你保证
为了捍卫你的歌声和光荣
我们将不惜献出自己的生命
河流啊，人类永恒的母亲
让我们再一次回到你的怀中
让我们再一次呼唤你的尊严和名字吧！

The faith and courage to go on living
I admit, mankind has inflicted grievous hurt on you

When we stand on the banks of dried-up rivers
Or look at your bodies suffering from pollution
Our repentant hearts feel a great grief
Believe it, rivers! We guarantee
That we will defend your song and your honor
We will not shrink from offering our lives
Ah rivers, eternal mother of humankind
Let us return once more to your embrace
Let us once again call out your honored names!

记忆中的小火车

——献给开远的小火车

那是一列
名副其实的小火车
它开过来的时候
司机的头探出窗外
他的喜悦
让所有看见他的人
都充满着少有的幸福
小火车要在无数个
有名字或者说没有名字的
站台上停留
那些赶集的人们
可以从这一个村寨
赶到另一个他们从未去过的集镇
火车是拥挤的
除了人之外，麻布口袋里的乳猪
发出哼哼的低吟
竹筐里的公鸡
认为它们刚从黑夜
又走到了一个充满希望的黎明
它们高昂的鸣叫此起彼伏
火车上还有穿着绣花服饰的妇女
她们三五成群
在那里掩着嘴窃窃私语
吸水烟筒的老人
仿佛永远蹲在一个黑暗的角落
水烟的味道弥漫在空气中
听他们说
那是一列名副其实的小火车
但是，既然，其实，不过
这似乎已经是
一件记忆里久远的事了

听他们说
那是一列名副其实的小火车
它就像一个传说中的故事
又像一条梦中的河流
然而这一切——
对于我们今天的回忆而言
是多么的温暖啊
尽管有时莫名的悲伤
也让我们的双眼饱含着泪水！

LITTLE TRAIN IN MY MEMORY

—Dedicated to a narrow-gauge train that has headed off to a faraway place . . .

It was a train that could only be described as "little"
As it pulled up to a stop
The engineer would lean out the window
His joy lit up the day
Of anyone who saw him
That narrow-gauge train stopped
At countless named and unnamed stations
People going to market
Could ride from a little hill stockade
To a market town they had never seen
The train was crowded, not just with people
But also with suckling pigs
That grunted in burlap bags
And roosters in bamboo cages
Crowing stridently here and there
Thinking they had escaped dark night
To enter a daylight of hope
Matrons in clothes chased with needlework
Were grouped together in threes and fives
Murmuring and covering their smiles
Old men smoking water pipes
Always seemed to hunker in dark corners
A smell of plug tobacco filled the air
I have been told it was a train
That merited the description "little"
Yet even so, in truth
There was something else about it
Something I can feel receding

I have been told it was a train
That could only be described as "little"
It was like a handed-down story
It was like a river in a dream
At times causing a twinge of sorrow
Yet all of this in our recollection
Even now remains so warm
It sometimes fills our eyes with tears

头发

——写给弗朗西斯科·林蒂尼

我说过我要写你的头发
那是在一只威尼斯的游船上

我说过我要写你的头发
它让我想起
西西里宁静而悠远的海浪
那里滚动着
三叶草与风信子的谜语

我说过我要写你的头发
它让我想起
地中海正午迷乱的阳光
大海洁白无瑕的积盐
它让我想起
所有时间之外
已经死去的空白
那里有鱼的轨迹，海鸟的历险
以及大理石上
那些预言宿命的纹路

我说过我要写你的头发
那是在一只威尼斯的游船上
我想我不会记错

HAIR

—For Francesco Lentini*

I said I wanted to write about your hair
That was on a gondola in Venice

I said I wanted to write about your hair
It reminded me of Sicily's peaceful, lissome waves
Within it tumbled riddles of clover and hyacinth

I said I wanted to write about your hair
It reminded me of disorienting sunlight
At noontime on the Mediterranean
And pure salt deposits from the sea
It made me think
Of dead blankness
Beyond all scales of time
Within it were haunts of fish, adventures of gulls
And the destiny-foretelling veins
Within a block of marble

I said I would write about your hair
That was on a gondola in Venice
I do not think my memory fails me

* Francesco Lentini was an Italian writer who chaired the judging committee for the Mondello International Literary Prize. After the poet met him in Venice, Lentini passed away.

记住这个时刻

在中国:
这是奔跑的时刻
这是选择的时刻
这是心中的道德被照亮的时刻
这是恐惧和从容不期而遇的时刻
这是沉默的词语失而复得的时刻
这是爱情将被等待证明的时刻
这是平凡之人牵动这个世界的时刻
这是领袖和人民共患难的时刻
这是微笑感召绝望的时刻
这是英雄呼唤奇迹的时刻
这是真理与谎言较量的时刻
这是卑鄙者无处藏身的时刻
这是人类面对灵魂独白的时刻
这是梦想被行动点燃的时刻
这是眼睛触动泪泉的时刻
这是黑暗预言光明的时刻
这是生命和死亡决战的时刻

记住吧
在中国:
这是一个刻骨铭心的时刻!

REMEMBER THIS TIME

In China
This is the time for flat-out sprinting
This is the time for making choices
This is the time for inner virtues to be blazoned at large
This is the time for fearfulness to learn composure
This is the time to revive our words that have fallen silent
This is the time when love waits to be proven
This is the time for ordinary people to affect the world
This is the time for leaders and citizens to throw in their lot together
This is the time for the smile that can rouse us from despair
This is the time for the hero who will summon miracles
This is the time for the contest of truth against lies
This is the time that gives scum nowhere to hide
This time confronts humankind with a soliloquy of the spirit
This is the time for dreams to be kindled by action
This is the time for eyes to tap the wellspring of tears
This is the time for darkness to foretell light
This is the time for life's all-out battle with death

Remember
Here in China
This era will etch its mark on your bones!

你是谁?

——献给为抗击"非典"而舍生忘死的人

你是谁?
戴着口罩, 穿着白衣
原谅我
说不出你的名字

但有一点
我想不会说错
你同样是父母的儿女
为了等你平安回来
你年迈的母亲
还在那里等待

或许是你的妻子
或许是你的丈夫
自从你离开家后
他们才发现
你在他们的生命中
是多么的重要
你就像一道彩虹
照亮了平凡的人生

你的孩子
给你写了一封信
看完信, 你竟泣不成声
在卡通故事里
寻找英雄的一代
第一次为自己的父母自豪

你是谁?
原谅我
说不出你的名字
但是我要告诉你
你是真正的天使
又是活生生的人
从来没有豪言壮语
你的爱才这样真实
我相信, 一定是因为你
今天的中国
才会在微笑中
双眼含着泪水!

WHO ARE YOU?

—For those who put their lives on the line during the SARS epidemic

Who are you?
Wearing surgical masks and white clothes
Forgive me, but
Your names do not come to my lips

Yet there is one thing
I can say for sure
You were children who had parents of your own
Your old mothers waited at home
Hoping for your safe return
And they are still waiting

Or perhaps it was your wife
Perhaps it was your husband
Your last departure from home
Was what it took for them to discover
Your importance in their lives
You are like a rainbow that came
To light up ordinary lives

Your children wrote you letters
That caused you to break out sobbing
In an era that looks to cartoons
For heroes worth admiring
It was time to be proud of their parents

Who were you?
Forgive me, but
Your names do not come to my lips
But let me tell you
You were true angels
Just as you were of flesh and blood
You never made grand pronouncements
Only thus could you show such genuine love
It must be because of you
That the China of today
When it smiles
Has tears in its eyes!

水和生命的发现

原谅我，大自然的水
我生命之中的水
或许是因为我们为世俗的生活而忙碌
或许是因为我们关于河流的记忆早已干枯
水！原谅我，我已经有很长时间
在梦想和现实的交错中将你遗忘
我空洞的思想犹如一口无底的井
在那黑暗的深处，我等待了很久
水！水！我要感谢你，在此时此刻
我的生命又在你的召唤下奇迹般地惊醒
是因为水，人类才抒写出了
那超越时空的历史和文明
同样也是因为水，我们这个蓝色的星球
才能把生命和水的礼赞
谦恭地奉献给了千千万万个生命
让我们就像敬畏生命一样敬畏一滴水吧
因为对人类而言，或者说对所有的生命而言
一滴水的命运或许就预言了这个世界的未来！

DISCOVERY OF WATER AND LIFE

Forgive me, water of the natural world
Water that I live by
Perhaps because we are busy with everyday life
Or because our memories of rivers have dried up
I ask forgiveness, water, for this long period
In a jumble of dreams and reality I forgot you
My hollow thinking is like a dried-up well
In these dark depths I have waited so long
Water! I am grateful to you this very moment
My life is roused by the miracle of your call
By the grace of water, mankind's pen has indited
A civilizing tale beyond time and space
Likewise because of water, on this blue planet
We can humbly offer, on behalf of all beings
Our praise for water and for life
Let us hold a drop of water in awe
Just as we hold life in awe . . .
Because for humankind, for every living thing
A water drop's fate foretells our world's future!

玫瑰祖母

——献给智利巴塔哥尼亚地区卡尔斯卡尔族群中的最后一位印第安人，她活到98岁，被誉为"玫瑰祖母"。

你是风中
凋零的最后一朵玫瑰
你的离去
曾让这个世界在瞬间
进入全部的黑暗
你在时间的尽头回望死去的亲人
就像在那浩瀚的星空里
倾听母亲发自摇篮的歌声
悼念你，玫瑰祖母
我就如同悼念一棵老树
在这无限的宇宙空间
你多么像一粒沙漠中的尘埃
谁知道明天的风
会把它吹向哪里？
我们为一个生命的消失而伤心
那是因为这个生命的基因
已经从大地的子宫中永远地死去
尽管这样，在这个星球的极地
我们依然会想起
杀戮、迫害、流亡、苦难
这些人类最古老的名词
玫瑰祖母，你的死是人类的灾难
因为对于我们而言
从今以后我们再也找不到一位
名字叫卡尔斯卡尔的印第安人
再也找不到你的族群
通往生命之乡的那条小路

GRANDMOTHER ROSSA

—Dedicated to the last Indian of the Kaweskar tribe in the Patagonia region of Chile. She lived to the age of ninety-eight and was known as "Grandmother Rossa."

You were a final rose
Withered in the wind
Your departure plunged the world
Into an instant of total darkness
At the end of time's corridor you gazed
Back upon dead relations
As if you were listening to a cradle song
Amid the starry heavens
I mourn you, Grandmother Rossa
As I would mourn an old tree
In these limitless cosmic reaches
How like a grain of desert sand you are
No one knows where tomorrow's wind
May carry you
We are saddened by a life's cessation
Because its genes have forever departed
From the uterus of the good earth
For my part, at the far end of this planet
I cannot help but think
Of slaughter, destruction, banishment, calamity
These words as ancient as humankind
Grandmother Rossa, your death is a human disaster
Because we who remain
Will never again find an Indian
Who bears the name Kaweskar
Never again can we find your tribe
And its little road leading to the land of life

羊驼

不知道为什么?
远远地看去
它的身影充满着人的神态
并不是今天它才站在这里
它曾无数次地穿过
时间和历史的隧道
尽管它的祖先, 在反抗压迫凌辱时
所选择的死亡方式从未改变
只有无言的抗争
以及岩石般的沉默
难怪何塞·马蒂这样讲
羊驼自己倒地而死
常常是为了捍卫生命的尊严
我还记得, 当我从安第斯山归来
有人问我印第安人的形象
我便会不假思索地说:
先生 ...... 是的 ...... 多么像 ......
你在秘鲁遇见过的羊驼!

ALPACA

I do not know why
When seen from a distance
Its figure has strongly human qualities
Today is not the first time it has stood here
More than once it has passed through
The gauntlet of time and history
Even though its ancestors
In resistance to oppression and torment
Never changed their chosen way of dying
Which could be naught but wordless opposition
And boulder-like silence
No wonder José Martí once said
When an alpaca falls over and dies
It is often in defense of life's dignity
I remember, upon returning from the Andes
When asked about the Indians' appearance
I would say without hesitation:
Sir, it is much like the alpacas
You may have seen in pictures of Peru!

印第安人的古柯

你已经被剥夺了一切
只剩下
口中咀嚼的古柯
我知道
你咀嚼它时
能看见祖先的模样
可以把心中的悲伤
倾述给复活的死亡
你还能在瞬间
把这个失去公正的世界
短暂地遗忘
然而，我知道
这一切对于你是多么地重要
虽然你已经一无所有
剩下的
就是口中的古柯
以及黑暗中的——希望！

AN INDIAN'S COCA

You have been deprived of everything
All you have left
Is the coca you chew
I know
When you chew it
You can see your ancestors' shapes
You can confide your heart's sorrow
To the resurrected dead
For a few short moments
You can let yourself forget
This world so lacking in justice
So I know
How important all this is to you
By now you have nothing
All that remains
Is the coca you chew
And amid the darkness . . . your hopes!

孔多尔神鹰

在科尔卡峡谷的空中
飞翔似乎将灵魂变重
因为只有在这样的高度
才能看清大地的伤口
你从诞生就在时间之上
当空气被坚硬的翅膀划破
没有血滴，只有羽毛的虚无
把词语抛进深渊
你是光和太阳的使者
把颂辞和祖先的呓语
送到每一位占卜者的齿间
或许这绵绵的群山
自古以来就是你神圣的领地
你见证过屠杀、阴谋和迫害
你是苦难中的记忆，那俯瞰
只能是一个种族的化身
至高无上的首领，印第安人的守护神
因为你的存在，在火焰和黑暗的深处
不幸多舛的命运才会在瞬间消失！

CONDOR, THE DIVINE BIRD*

In the skies over Colca Canyon
Flight appears to make the soul heavy
Because only at this height
Does it command a view of the land's wounds
Since birth you have been above time
When sturdy wings slice through air
There is no blood, only feathery emptiness
To hurl words out over an abyss
You are messenger of the sun and its rays
You bring hymns and ancestral chants
To the lips of a diviner
Perhaps those far-stretching ridgelines
Have been your sacred precinct for ages
You have witnessed slaughter, dark plots, harsh trials
You are memory in dire times, your commanding vision
Could only belong to the avatar of a race
Highest chieftain, guardian of the Indians
Only by your existence, deep in fire and darkness
Can a malign fate be wiped away in an instant!

* The condor is the great bird of the Andes; it is honored and revered by the Indians.

我怀念

我怀念诞生，我怀念死亡
当一轮月亮升起在吉勒布特高高的白杨树梢
在山岗之上，在群山之上，那里皎洁的月光已将蓝色的天幕照亮
那是记忆复活之前的土地
我的白天和夜晚都如同最初的神话和传说
在破晓的曙光中，毕阿史拉则赞颂过的太阳
像一个圣者用它的温暖
唤醒了我的旷野和神灵，同样也唤醒了
我羊毛披毡下梦境正悄然离去的族人
我怀念，我至死也怀念那样的夜晚
火塘闪着微暗的火，亲人们昏昏欲睡
讲述者还在不停地述说......。我不知道谁能忘记！
我的怀念，是光明和黑暗的隐喻
在河流消失的地方，时间的光芒始终照耀着过去
当威武的马队从梦的边缘走过，那闪动白银般光辉的
马鞍终于消失在词语的深处。此时我看见了他们
那些我们没有理由遗忘的先辈和智者，其实
他们已经成为了这片土地自由和尊严的代名词
我崇拜我的祖先，那是因为
他们曾经生活在一个英雄时代，每一部
口述史诗都传颂着他们的英名
当然，我歌唱过幸福，那是因为我目睹
远走他乡的孩子又回到了母亲身旁
是的，你也看见过我哭泣，那是因为我的羊群
已经失去了丰盈的草地，我不知道明天它们会去哪里？
我怀念，那是因为我的忧伤，绝不仅仅是忧伤本身
那是因为作为一个人
我时常把那逝去的一切美好怀念！

GLOWING EMBERS IN THE FIREPLACE

I relive the births, I relive the deaths
When the moon's orb rises to the tops of the poplars
In Jjile Bute, over the ranged mountains, over dark places
Heaven's blue canopy is lit by silvery beams
That was my land, before memory was resurrected
Day and night passed as in a primal myth or legend
As dawn's light broke, the sun that Biashylazzi praised*
Was like a sage, using its tenderness
To waken my moorlands and nature spirits
Just as it wakened my tribesmen
From fading dreams beneath wool capes
Until death I will think fondly of those nights
When the fire glowed and my loved ones nodded
As the storyteller kept up his tale . . . Who could forget?
Remembrance is a play of light and darkness
Time has rays to illumine a vanished river
As a column of riders approaches along a dream's edge
The silvery brightness of saddles disappears
Deep into a word string, whereupon I see them
Elders and wise men we are not justified in forgetting
In fact, they signify truth and dignity on this land
I worship my ancestors because
They lived in an era of heroes
Each oral epic retells their glory
Of course I have sung of my happiness at seeing
Those prodigals who returned to their mothers' sides
And if you have seen me weep, it is for my flock
Now that rich pastures are gone, where will it go?
I think back, not to dwell on sad losses
Just being human I am drawn
To relive all beautiful bygone things!

* Biashylazzi was a ritualist and culture-bearer famous in the history of the Nuosu people.

火焰与词语

我把词语掷入火焰
那是因为只有火焰
能让我的词语获得自由
而我也才能将我的全部一切
最终献给火焰
（当然包括肉体和灵魂）
我像我的祖先那样
重复着一个古老的仪式
是火焰照亮了所有的生命
同样是火焰
让我们看见了死去的亲人
当我把词语
掷入火焰的时候
我发现火塘边的所有族人
正凝视着永恒的黑暗
在它的周围，没有叹息
只有雪族十二子的面具
穿着节日的盛装列队而过
他们的口语，如同沉默
那些格言和谚语滑落在地
却永远没有真实的回声
让我们惊奇的是，在那些影子中
真实已经死亡，而时间
却活在另一个神圣的地域
没有选择，只有在这样的夜晚
我才是我自己
我才是诗人吉狄马加
我才是那个不为人知的通灵者
因为只有在这个时刻
我舌尖上的词语和火焰
才能最终抵达我们伟大种族母语的根部！

WORDS OF FIRE

I throw phrases into flames
Because only flames
Can give my phrases freedom
And only thus can I offer
All that I am to the fire
(both flesh and spirit, of course)
In the way of my ancestors
I repeat an ancient verse
Flame illumines living things
Just as it lets us see
Our departed kindred
As I throw my words into flames
I notice all my fellow Nuosu gazing
With bated breath into timeless darkness
Where the twelve sons of the Snow Tribe*
File by in their masks and robes
Their speech is one with the silence
Proverbs and sayings have slid to earth
Never raising an echo in the real world
It shocks me that reality is dead
For these shadows, yet time lives on
In their sacred, alternate realm
When else but on such an evening
Can I be myself
Namely the poet Jidi Majia
The seer few people know
Because only at this moment
Can these flames, these words on my lips
Reach to the root of my native tongue!

* A Nuosu myth says that living things originated from the twelve sons of the Snow Tribe

一种声音

——我的创作谈

我写诗，是因为我出生的那个日子，显然不能靠前，更不能靠后，恰好就是一九六一年六月二十三日。

我写诗，是因为我本身就是一个偶然。

我写诗，是因为我的父亲是彝族，我的母亲也是彝族。他们都是神人支呷阿鲁的子孙。

我写诗，是因为我的爷爷长得异常英俊，我的奶奶却有些丑。

我写诗，是因为我生活在一个叫昭觉的小城，那里有许多彝人，还有许多汉人。他们好像非常熟悉，又好像非常陌生。

我写诗，是因为在少年时我曾被别人伤害。

我写诗，是因为我害羞，然而我又渴望表达。

我写诗，是因为在一个夏天我读了巴金的《海的梦》。

我写诗，是因为我很早就意识到死。

我写诗，是因为我的忧虑超过了我的欢乐。

我写诗，是因为我有一个汉族保姆，她常常让我相信，在她的故乡有人可以变成白虎，每到傍晚就要去撞别人家的门。

我写诗，是因为我异想天开。

我写诗，是因为我会讲故事。

我写诗，是因为我的叔叔来城里告诉我，他的家中要送鬼， 说是需要一头羊八只鸡。

我写诗，是因为我两次落入水中，但都大难不死。

我写诗，是因为我学会了游泳。

我写诗，是因为我相信万物有灵。

我写诗，是因为一九七八年我有幸考入了西南民族学院中文系，在那里熟读了屈原和米哈依尔•肖洛霍夫。

我写诗，是因为我知道，我的父亲属于古候部落，我的母亲属于曲涅部落。他们都非常神秘。

我写诗，是因为我无法解释自己。

ONE KIND OF VOICE

—About my poetry writing

I write poems because my birth could have happened no sooner
and clearly no later than the exact day of June 23, 1961.
I write poems because I myself am a random event.
I write poems because my parents are both of the Nuosu ethnicity;
they are descendants of Zhyge Alu, the divine hero of the Nuosu.
I write poems because my grandfather was especially handsome,
but my grandmother was a bit ugly.
I write poems because I live in a small city called Zhaojue, where
many Nuosu people and Han people live together. They seem
quite familiar with each other, yet they also seem strange to each
other.
I write poems because I was hurt by someone as a child.
I write poems because I always feel shy, yet I wish to express myself.
I write poems because one summer I read a book by Ba Jin entitled
Dream of the Sea.
I write poems because I was aware of death very early.
I write poems because my worries always outweigh my joys.
I write poems because I had a Han Chinese nanny who often
claimed there was a man in her hometown who could transform
into a white tiger, and the tiger used to push open people's gates
at night.
I write poems because I often indulge in the wildest fantasies.
I write poems because I am good at telling stories.
I write poems because my uncle once came to my house in the city
and said he planned to exorcise the ghosts from his house, for
which he needed one sheep and eight cocks.
I write poems because I sank twice into water over my head, but
escaped death both times.
I write poems because I have learned to swim well.
I write poems because I believe all creatures on earth have souls.
I write poems because I was admitted in 1978 to Southwest
Minorities College, where I read the works of Qu Yuan and
Mikhail Sholokhov.

I write poems because I know my father is of the Guhou clan
and my mother of the Qunie clan, both of which seem full of
mystery to me.
I write poems because I am unable to explain myself.

我写诗，是因为我想分清什么是善，什么又是恶。我崇拜卡夫卡和陀思妥耶夫斯基。

我写诗，是因为我的语言中枢中混杂有彝语和汉语，奇怪的是它们最初都是象形文字。

我写诗，是因为有一个 《星星》 诗刊，他们曾集中发表过我的诗。

我写诗，是因为我承受着多种文化的冲突。有什么办法呢，我就生活在这样一个地带。

我写诗，是因为我只要听见故乡的歌谣，就会两眼含满泪水。

我写诗，是因为有人对彝族和红黄黑三种色彩并不了解。

我写诗，是因为我母亲的口语十分幽默，而且格外生动。

我写诗，是因为在没有人的时候我无端地想哭。

我写诗，是因为我在九岁时，由于不懂事打了我的妹妹，现在想起来还异常惭愧。

我写诗，是因为我遇到了许多人，他们不好也不坏。

我写诗，是因为我的部族的祭司给我讲述了彝人的历史，掌 故、风俗、人情、天文和地理。

我写诗，是因为我们生活在一个有核原子的时代，我们更加渴望的是人类的和平。

我写诗，是因为我们在探索生命的意义，我们在渴望同自然有一种真正的交流，这种神的交流当然是来自心灵而不是表面。

我写诗，是因为多少年来，我一直想同自己古老的历史对话，可是我却常常成了哑巴。

我写诗，是因为渴望表达自己真实的感情和心灵的感受。我发现有一种神秘的力量在感召着我。

I write poems because I wish to distinguish good and evil. I worship Kafka and Dostoevsky.
I write poems because Chinese and Nuosu are mixed in the central nervous system of my language; strangely enough, they were both originally written in pictographic scripts.
I write poems because there was a poetry journal called *Stars* that published a special section on my poems.
I write poems because I have to bear the clash of various cultures. There is no way around it, considering the region where I live.
I write poems because I shed tears whenever I hear the folk songs of my native place.
I write poems because a lot of people don't know the underlying meanings of red, yellow, and black—the three basic colors of the Nuosu.*
I write poems because my mother's spoken language is lively and rich in humor.
I write poems because when no one is around, I feel like weeping for no reason.
I write poems because when I was a child of nine, I thoughtlessly beat my younger sister, and even now I feel shame and remorse over it.
I write poems because I have encountered many people who were neither good nor bad.
I write poems because a Nuosu sage gave me instruction in the history, lore, customs, sensibility, astronomy, and geography of our people.
I write poems because we live in an era of nuclear weapons, but what we wish for most is world peace.
I write poems because we have explored the meaning of life, and we long for genuine interchange with nature; of course, such a spiritual connection comes from deep in the heart, not from the surface.
I write poems because I have long wished to hold a dialogue with my people's ancient history, yet I often fall mute.

I write poems because I wish to voice my true feelings and the stirrings in my soul; I can feel a mysterious force drawing me onward.

* In the Nuosu worldview, red is connected with fire, and fire is associated with the Torch Festival, the pivotal festival of the year at the spring equinox, when stars that were getting farther away now begin to approach the earth again. Hence the red of fire represents life's power to be renewed again and again. Because no invocation or scripture reading is complete without a fire in which green boughs are burned, red also ties to ceremonies performed by the *bimo* priests. Yellow is associated with the sun's power to make things grow. It also relates to the eagle, embodiment of the sun's power, which conceived a child with the ancestress Pumo Hniyyr (mother of the Nuosu culture hero Zhyge Alu), as told in the *Book of Origins*.

我写诗，是因为希望它具有彝人的感情和色彩，同时又希望它属于大家。
我写诗，是因为我天生就有一种使命感，可是我从来没有为这一点而感到不幸。
我写诗，是因为对人类的理解不是一句空洞无物的话，它需要我们去拥抱和爱。对人的命运的关注，哪怕是对一个小小的部落作深刻的理解，它也是会有人类性的。对此我深信不疑。
我写诗，是因为人类居住在这个不断发生着变化的大地上，人类面对万物和自身，时时刻刻都在寻找其本质和规律。
我写诗，是因为在现代文明和古老传统的反差中，我们灵魂中的阵痛是任何一个所谓文明人永远无法体会得到的。我们的父辈常常陷入一种从未有过的迷惘。
我写诗，是因为我相信，忧郁的色彩是一个内向深沉民族的灵魂显像。它很早很早以前就潜藏在这个民族心灵的深处。
我写诗，是因为我相信，人死了安息在土地和天空之间。
我写诗，是因为我的父亲是神枪手，他一生正直、善良，只 要他喝醉了酒，我便会听他讲述自己的过去。泪水会溢出我的眼睛。
我写诗，是因为我的父亲已经死了，我非常怀念他。这是一个真正的人，大写的人。
我写诗，是因为我在意大利的罗马，看见一个人的眼里充满了绝望，于是我相信人在这个世界的痛苦并没有什么两样。
我写诗，是因为我站在钢筋和水泥的阴影之间，我被分割成两半。
我写诗，是因为我在城市喧嚣的舞厅中想找回我丢失的口弦。

我写诗，是因为我想让人能够更多地彼此了解。
我写诗，是因为在这个世界上，有一百个女人爱我，但只有一个女人承认在梦中背叛过我。
我写诗，是因为我想告诉自己，同时又告诉别人，人活着的时间非常短暂。

I write poems because I hope they will have a Nuosu emotional coloring while belonging to everyone.

I write poems because I have an inborn sense of mission, yet I have never felt this to be a misfortune.

I write poems because I think human understanding is not empty talk; it requires us to open our arms and give love. To show concern for people's fate, if only by learning about a small tribe in depth, makes us more human. This is my unshakable belief.

I write poems because we humans live on this earth's constantly changing surface; in dealing with ourselves and other living things, we seek to grasp laws and inner substance.

I write poems because the gulf between modernity and ancient tradition has racked our souls with pain that no person from a so-called civilized society will ever experience. Our fathers' generation was often plunged into an unprecedented state of anomie.

I write poems because it seems to me that the spirit of our introspective, ruminative tribe is shown outwardly in a melancholy color. For a long time, this color has been harbored deep in our souls.

I write poems because I believe that after death, a person rests in peace between land and sky.

I write poems because my father was a marksman; he was honest and kindhearted all his life; when drunk, he would tell stories of his past, which made tears quietly well up in my eyes.

I write poems because my father has died and I miss him dearly; he was a true man, a man writ large.

I write poems because once in Rome I saw a man whose eyes were filled with despair; thus I believe that people around the world do not differ in their pain.

I write poems because I feel cut in half whenever I stand in the shadow of steel rods and concrete.

I write poems because I still want to find my lost mouth harp in the noisy dance halls of the city.

I write poems because I want to help people understand each other better.

I write poems because in this world, one hundred women love me, but only one of them recognizes that she has betrayed me in dreams.

I write poems because I want to tell myself and others that life is very short.

我写诗，是因为哥伦比亚有一个加西亚·马尔克斯，智利有一个巴波罗·聂鲁达，塞内加尔有一个桑戈尔，墨西哥有一个奥克塔维奥·帕斯。
我写诗，是因为在某种时候我会成为众矢之的。
我写诗，是因为我常常想像巫师那样，说出超现实主义的语言。
我写诗，是因为我一直无法理解"误会"这个词。
我写诗，是因为我别无选择，似乎干这一行更合适。

I write poems because Colombia has a man named García Márquez,
Chile has a man named Pablo Neruda, Senegal has a man named
L. S. Senghor, and Mexico has a man named Octavio Paz.
I write poems because at times I am likely to be a target of
widespread attack.
I write poems because I often wish to utter surrealistic words, in the
manner of a wizard.
I write poems because I have never understood the word
"misunderstanding."
I write poems because I have no other choice, and it seems I am
suited for this line of work.

圣殿般的雪山

——献给东方伟大的山脉昆仑山

圣殿般的雪山
在可可西里的暮色上
燃烧着金色的火焰
我呼吸秋天无边的旷野
遥望星群以及天空的幻象
如何坠入黑暗的母腹

我的思想和欲望，正在变轻
我知道，这是最后的选择
当我的舌尖传颂着神灵的赞辞
远方的大海停止了蓝色的渴望

我们是真正的雪族十二子
刚刚从英雄的挽歌中复活
只有在这太阳永恒的领地
鸟的影子，生命的轮回
才能让我们的记忆变成永恒

传说在山巅闪耀着宁静的光辉
此时，我就像一个祭献者
泪流满面，尽管一无所有
因为我已经承诺我命运中的箴言
都将倾诉给黄昏的使者

我发现我的灵魂在寻找一个方向
穿过了山谷，穿过了透明的空气
穿过了原野，穿过了自由的王国
我看见它，像一只金色的神鹰
最终抵达了人类光明的入口！

HOLY SNOW MOUNTAIN

—Dedicated to the Kunlun Mountains, one of the great ranges of the Orient

Tabernacle of snowy peaks
And in Kekexili's oncoming dusk
The sky is lit with golden torches
I draw breaths of autumn wilderness
And watch the starry veil of Maya fall
Into the darkness of the mother's belly

My thoughts and wishes are buoyed up
I know my final chance has arrived
My tongue sends forth praise of holy spirits
While blue yearnings for distant seas subside

Truly we stem from the Snow Tribe's dozen sons
Resurrected of late from a requiem for heroes
Only here, in sunlight's eternal domain
Will the shadow of a bird, the cycle of life
Render the stuff of memory eternal

The peak glows serenely, as stories tell
At this moment I resemble a celebrant
With nothing to offer but the tears on my face
And my lifelong credo, to which I give voice
Confiding it to messengers of twilight

I find that my spirit seeks direction
Passing through valleys, through pristine air
Through a broad plain, a land of freedom
Far off I see it, like a sacred golden garuda
At last reaching mankind's entranceway of light!

嘉那嘛呢石上的星空

是谁在召唤着我们?
石头, 石头, 石头
那神秘的气息都来自于石头
它的光亮在黑暗的心房
它是六字箴言的羽衣
它用石头的形式
承载着另一种形式

每一块石头都在沉落
仿佛置身于时间的海洋
它的回忆如同智者的归宿
始终在生与死的边缘上滑行
它的倾诉在坚硬的根部
象无色的花朵
悄然盛开在不朽的殿堂
它是恒久的纪念之碑
它用无言告诉无言
它让所有的生命相信生命
石头在这里
就是一本奥秘的书
无论是谁打开了首页
都会目睹过去和未来的真相
这书中的每一个词语都闪着光
雪山在其中显现
光明穿越引力, 蓝色的雾霭
犹如一个飘渺的音阶

STARFIELDS OVER THE GANA *MANE* CAIRN

What voice cries out to summon us
In stone after stone after stone?*
Out of the stones comes mysterious breath
It is radiance in the heart's dark chambers
It is the four-word mantra's feathered cape
With the form of stones as a vehicle
It carries another kind of form

Each of these stones is sinking
As if to the bottom of time's ocean
Its memory is like a refuge for the wise
Forever gliding at the edge of birth and death
At its obdurate root is a confession
Like a colorless flower
Blooming unseen in an immortal shrine
It is a plaque of enduring tribute
Giving its wordless message to the wordless
Letting all living things believe in life
The stones at this site
Are an arcane book
Whoever turns to the first page
Sees past and future in their true guise
Each word holds beams of light
Wherein snowy mountains are manifest
Rays pass through gravity and bluish mist
Forming wispy layers like musical scales

* This poem was written after a visit to the famous cairn of *mane* stones in Xinzhai, close to the capital of Yushu Prefecture in Qinghai Province. The first stones were laid by Duoren Rinpoche, founder of the Jiegu Monastery in Yushu. The cairn bears the name "Gana," referring to the Central Plain of China, which was used as a second name for Duoren Rinpoche because he had spent time there.

The cairn took shape over more than three centuries, built in the form of a wall one hundred meters long and two meters high. It is estimated that 2.5 billion stones were used to build it. The stones are called *mane* stones because the mantra *om mane padme hum* is carved on them. Some of the stones bear sutra texts.

According to Tibetan beliefs, suffering in the present life lays a foundation for blessedness in the next life. Stones carved with *om mane padme hum* are a symbol of steadfastness in adversity; they are also a concrete manifestation of faith in the mantra's efficacy. In the aftermath of the Yushu earthquake of 2010, several thousand new *mane* stones were laid at the cairn as a memorial to earthquake victims.

In this poem, the poet voices a wish to speak on behalf of Gesar, a traditional hero of the Tibetan people.

每一块石头都是一滴泪
在它晶莹的幻影里
苦难变得轻灵，悲伤没有回声
它是唯一的通道
它让死去的亲人，从容地踏上
一条伟大的旅程
它是英雄葬礼的真正序曲
在那神圣的超度之后
山峦清晰无比，牛羊犹如光明的使者
太阳的赞辞凌驾于万物
树木已经透明，意识将被遗忘
此刻，只有那一缕缕白色的炊烟
为我们证实
这绝不是虚幻的家园
因为我们看见
大地没有死去，生命依然活着
黎明时初生婴儿的啼哭
是这片复活了的土地
献给万物最动人的诗篇

嘉那嘛呢石，我不了解
这个世界上还有没有比你更多的石头
因为我知道
你这里的每一块石头
都是一个不容置疑的个体生命
它们从诞生之日起
就已经镌刻着祈愿的密码
我真的不敢去想象
二十五亿块用生命创造的石头
在获得另一种生命形式的时候
这其中到底还隐含着什么？

嘉那嘛呢石，你既是真实的存在
又是虚幻的象征
我敢肯定，你并不是为了创造奇迹
才来到这个世界
因为只有对每一个个体生命的热爱
石头才会象泪水一样柔软
词语才能被微风千百次的吟诵
或许，从这个意义上而言
嘉那嘛呢石，你就是真正的奇迹

Each stone is a teardrop
Within that light-suffused shape
Suffering turns buoyant, sorrow's echo fades
It is the only passageway
Wherein the beloved dead can be lulled
To embark on the grandest journey
It is the true prelude to a hero's burial
And after holy deliverance from limbo
Ridgelines show beautiful distinctness
Grazing beasts resemble messengers of light
The sun's vatic rays hold sway over earthly life
Trees are crystalline, random notions fall away
Whereupon those columns of kitchen smoke
Are all we need to prove
This homeland is no illusion
For we can see
The good earth has not died, life goes on
The cry of an infant born at dawn
Is the most stirring hymn to life on earth
That our resurrected land could sing

Ah, Gana *Mane* Cairn, I know no place on earth
Where a greater assemblage of stones could be found
Knowing as I do
That each of your stones
Carries life undeniable
From birth each stone was inscribed
With the code words of prayer
If such life force can even be imparted
To two billion stones, I dare not imagine
What heights and depths it could harbor
Should it achieve a different form of existence

Gana *Mane* Cairn, you have genuine existence
You are also an illusory symbol
Even so, I know you did not come into this world
As a display of miraculous handiwork
For only by those who live and love, one by one
Can stones be made soft and tender like tears
Can a phrase be chanted all day by wind
O great cairn, in this sense of the word
I will grant that you are a miracle

因为是那信仰的力量
才创造了这超越时间和空间的永恒

沿着一个方向，嘉那嘛呢石
这个方向从未改变，就象刚刚开始
这是时间的方向，这是轮回的方向
这是白色的方向，这是慈航的方向
这是原野的方向，这是天空的方向
因为我已经知道
只有从这里才能打开时间的入口

嘉那嘛呢石，在子夜时分
我看见天空降下的甘露
落在了那些新摆放的嘛呢石上
我知道，这几千块石头
代表着几千个刚刚离去的生命
嘉那嘛呢石，当我瞩望你的瞬间
你的夜空星群灿烂
庄严而神圣的寂静依偎着群山
远处的白塔正在升高
无声的河流闪动着白银的光辉
无限的空旷如同燃烧的凯旋
这时我发现我的双唇正离开我的身躯
那些神授的语言
已经破碎成无法描述的记忆
于是，我仿佛成为了一个格萨尔传人
我的灵魂接纳了神秘的暗示

嘉那嘛呢石，请你塑造我
是你把全部的大海注入了我的心灵
在这样一个蓝色的夜晚
我就是一只遗忘了思想和自我的海螺
此时，我不是为吹奏而存在
我已是另一个我，我的灵魂和思想
已经成为了这片高原的主人
嘉那嘛呢石，请倾听我对你的吟唱
虽然我不是一个合格的歌者
但我的双眼已经泪水盈眶！

2011年3月16日

By the power of faith at work here
Something beyond time and space was created

Gana *Mane* Cairn, in you one follows a direction
A direction that has never changed, as if just begun
It is the direction of time, of reincarnation
It is the direction of whiteness, of a compassionate journey
It is the direction of wilderness, the direction of sky
Which I now know is the sole way
To open the gateway of duration

O great cairn, at the midnight hour
I see sweet dew descending from the sky
To bedeck these newly laid stones
I know that each of these stones
Stands for a just-departed life
Gana *Mane* Cairn, now as I gaze on you
Star clusters sparkle in the sky above
A grave and holy silence lies over the mountains
A distant white tower is rising up
Silver lights twinkle along a silent river
Like a victory march blazing, through great expanses
My lips seem to be estranged from my body
Language imparted by divine powers
Dwindles to elusive fragments of memory
Yet I feel favored to carry Gesar's message
My soul opens to mystic intimations

Gana *Mane* Cairn, please shape me
It is you that has poured an ocean into my heart
In the deep blueness of night
I am a conch shell, emptied of selfish thoughts
I no longer live just to play an instrument
My self is another self, the thoughts in my soul
Belong to the sovereign presence of this highland
Great cairn, please hear the words I intone for you
Although I am not qualified as a bard
My eyes are brimming with tears!

March 16, 2011

我把我的诗写在天空和大地之间

我把我的诗写在天空和大地之间
那是因为，只能在这辽阔的天宇
我才能书写这样的诗句
其实，在这个奇迹诞生之前，时间的影子
也曾千百次地穿越我们
我们是自然之子，是雪豹的兄弟
是羚羊的化身，是尊贵的冠冕
是那天幕上一颗永恒的祖母绿
也许那是另一个我，像一个酋长
青铜的额头上缀满着星星的宝石
我想写，当我重返大地的子宫
我看见我的诗，如同黄金和白银的饰带
虽然没有声音，却泪珠闪烁
原谅我，巴颜喀拉的诸神
今天我在黎明前就穿着盛装苏醒
并不是像往日那样参加你的仪式，而我的
歌唱却正在成为人类幸福的赞歌

我把我的诗写在天空和大地之间
那是因为，神鹰的记忆是唯一的高度
当光明和黑暗在星球的海洋里转换方向
亘古不变的太阳，又是谁加冕于你
让你成为真正的无冕之王。万物的首领
就在这个梦想变成现实的底部
无数的灵魂都曾将信仰的火草点燃
劈开黑色的沟壑，渴望那一条条深沉的河流
所有的生命都没有目的，我们一直在等待
我们等待的石头依然是石头
我们等待时间被时间证明后还是时间
我们等待一个结束
其实是另一个结束之前的开始
我们的等待在杀死等待
让词汇的意义相反，让缄默呐喊
让刚刚诞生的生命，死于一千年前的今天
我们的庆典，不是为了肉体孤独的那一部分
我们是为那光明和温暖的使者已经来临
他已经吹响了神圣的号角，像一只独角兽
站在那群山护卫的城郭上

I WRITE MY POEMS BETWEEN SKY AND EARTH

I write my poems between sky and earth
Because only with the firmament above me
Can I find the poetic lines I want
In fact, before this miracle can happen, time's shadow
Must pass through us hundreds of times
We are children of nature, brothers of the snow leopard
Avatar of the highland antelope, the crown of dignity
A tile of eternal turquoise in the sky's canopy
Perhaps that is another self, like a chieftain
His bronze forehead bedecked with gems of stars
I want to write them, and upon returning to earth's womb
To see my poems, like gold and silver buckles
Though voiceless, still showing that teardrop sparkle . . .
Forgive me, gods of Mount Bayan Har*
Today I keep a predawn vigil in my finest clothes
Not to join in your rituals as before, but so that
My poem can be a hymn to human blessings

I write my poems between sky and earth
Because memory of the thunderbird is my sole altitude
While light and dark alternate on the planet's oceans
Who was it who enthroned you, eternal sun
Making you our uncrowned king? Sovereign of all things
Down in the fundament of his dream-turned-reality
Countless souls once lit the bundled straw of faith
Cleaving black chasms, thirsting for deep-seated rivers
We living things lack goals; we have been waiting
The stones we waited for are stones, as always
The time we await has been proven to be temporal
We wait for a conclusion
In truth it will commence a different conclusion
Our waiting slaughters waiting
It turns meanings of words on end, makes silence cry out
Causes new life to die, due to a long-ago today
Our festival is not for the lonely part of the flesh
But to greet a messenger of light and warmth
He has sounded a clarion call, like a unicorn appearing
On the wall of encircling mountains

---

* Mount Bayan Har is a famous mountain on the Qinghai-Tibet Plateau.

我把我的诗写在天空和大地之间
那是因为，我的诞生就是诞生
而我的死亡却不是死亡
那是因为，我从遥远的未来返回
我没有名字，我的名字就是这片高原的名字
我把我的诗写在天空和大地之间
我为红色的理想呼唤。我为红色的颜色
添加更多的红色。因为我早已热泪盈眶！
我知道，那是一群人类的英雄
他们全部的壮举，并不为世人所知晓
是他们打碎了一个远古的神话，而就在
这个神话的碎片还没有站起来的时候
他们又创造了一个属于今天的神话
我不能一一说出他们的名字，就如同我这个歌者
遗忘了自己的名字
他们属于一个伟大的集体。他们高尚的灵魂
已经嵌入了这片土地的身躯
我相信，没有一句诗能全部概括他们创造的伟业
尽管如此，我还是要为他们写出这篇赞美的颂辞！

2011年12月12日

I write my poems between sky and earth
Because my birth is only a birth
But my death will not be death
Because I have come back from the future
I have no name; my name is the name of this plateau
I write my poems between heaven and earth
At the summons of red ideals. To the color red
Let me add redness, for it has filled my eyes with tears
I know those path-breakers are heroes of humanity
The extent of their deeds is beyond this era's knowing
For they broke apart a myth from ancient times
Then before that myth could regain its footing
They created a myth that belongs to today
I cannot list their names, just as my own name
Is forgotten in the act of singing
They belong to a noble cohort, their exalted souls
Have been embedded in the body of this land
I admit that no lines of poetry can sum up their legacy
Even so, I wish to write this paean in their praise

December 12, 2011

那是我们的父辈

——献给诗人艾梅•塞泽尔

昨晚我想到了艾梅•塞泽尔，想到了一个令人尊敬的人
昨晚我想到了所有返乡的人
他们忧伤的目光充满着期待
艾梅•塞泽尔，我真的不知道，这条回乡的道路究竟有多长？
但是我却知道，我们必须回去
无论路途是多么的遥远！
艾梅•塞泽尔，我已经在你黑色的意识里看见了
你对于这个世界的悲悯之情
因为凡是亲近过你的灵魂，看见过你的泪眼的生命个体
无论他们是黑种人、白种人还是黄种人
都会相信你全部的诗歌，就是一个种族离去和归来的记忆
艾梅•塞泽尔，非洲的饥饿直到今天还张着绝望的嘴
我曾经相信过上帝的公平，然而在这个星球上
还生活着许许多多不幸的人们
公平和正义却从未降临在他们的头上
艾梅•塞泽尔，因为你我想到了我们彝人的先辈和故土
想到了一望无际的群山和一条条深沉的河流
还有那些瓦板屋。成群的牛羊。睁大眼睛的儿童
原谅我，到如今我才知道，在逝去的先辈面前
我们的生存智慧已经褪化，我们的梦想
早已消失在所谓文明的天空
毕阿史拉则的语言在陌生钢铁和水泥的季节里临界死亡
而我们离出发的地点已经越来越远
是的，艾梅•塞泽尔，我为我的父辈而骄傲
因为他们还在童年的时候，就能熟背古老的
格言和劝解部族纷争的谚语
他们的眼睛像鹰一样犀利
他们自信的目光却又像湖泊一样平静

OF OUR FATHERS' GENERATION

—For Aimé Césaire*

Last night I thought about Aimé Césaire, about a man worthy of my respect
Last night I thought about people who return to their native place
I see anticipation light up their sad gaze
Aimé Césaire, how long the homeward road is, truly I do not know
But I do know I need to make that journey back
However far that road may stretch!
Aimé Césaire, through your black consciousness I have seen
A compassionate vision of the world
Anyone who has felt your soul's nearness, seen your tearful eyes
Any person of the black, white, or yellow race would affirm
Your poems carry a race's memory of parting and return
Aimé Césaire, hunger in Africa even now opens its despairing mouth
I once believed in the Lord's fairness, but many are the unfortunate
Eking out lives here on this planet, upon whom
Justice and fairness have never alighted
Aimé Césaire, you remind me of my Nuosu forebears and our land
I think of ranged mountains, as far as the eye can see, and those deep-set rivers
Those tile and wattle houses, herds dotting the land, wide-eyed children
Forgive me, now I realize, standing before my departed elders
That our wits and know-how have regressed, and our dreams
Have vanished into so-called civilization's sky
Biashylazzi's language is near death, in a season of cement and steel
We travel ever farther from our point of departure
Yes, Aimé Césaire, I am proud of my father's generation
Because in childhood they knew ancient sayings by heart
They knew proverbs for urging peace among clans
Their eyes had eagle-eyed sharpness
Their confident gaze was like a placid mountain lake

---

* Aimé Césaire (1913–2008), a black poet, humanitarian, and politician from Martinique, proposed the idea of *Négritude* and was a lifelong proponent of blacks' need to regain self-esteem and learn their roots. He was also the founding figure of literature in Martinique. His *Notebook of a Return to My Native Land* is a seminal work of black literature.

他们的女人是最矜持的女人，每一圈朵啰荷舞的身姿
都能让大地滚动着白银的光辉
那是我们的父辈：喜欢铿亮的快枪
珍爱达里阿宗那样的骏马，相信神圣的传统，坚信祖先的力量
那无与伦比讲述故事的能力，来自于部族千百年仪式的召唤
他们热爱生命，更重要的是他们不怕死亡
是的，艾梅•塞泽尔，我的父辈从未失去过对身份和价值的认同
他们同样为自己的祖先充满着自豪。因为在他们口诵的家谱上
已经记载着无数智者和德古的名字
他们赤着脚。像豹子一样敏捷。具备羚羊的速度
在征战的时候，他们跳跃于茫茫的群山和峡谷
那麂子般的触觉，能穿透黎明前的雾霭
他们是鹰和虎豹的儿子
站在那高高的山顶，他们头上的英雄结，就是一束燃烧的火焰
是盐和看不见的山风塑造了矫健的形体。他们从诞生之日起
就把自由和尊严埋进了自己的骨骼。他们是彝人在自己独有的
创造史诗的时代之后
留存下来的、最后的、伟大的自然之子和英雄的化身
艾梅•塞泽尔，你没有死去，你的背影仍然在返乡的道路上前行
你不会孤独。与你同行的是这个世界上成千上万的返乡人和那些永远渴望故土的灵魂！

2011年9月5日

Their women were the haughtiest; each round of their *dulohxo* dance
Could spin an aura of silvery brilliance
Our fathers' generation liked to polish their repeating rifles
They loved spirited horses, believed in sacred traditions and the ancestors' power
The stories they told had wonderful power, for they were tied to an ageless chain of ceremonies
They loved life, but more importantly they did not fear death
Yes, Aimé Césaire, my father's generation never lost identity and values
Likewise they were proud of their forebears, learned genealogies by heart
To hand down the memory of admirable, sagely men
They ran barefoot, quick as panthers, swift as antelopes
On campaign they skipped along canyons, over haze-hidden mountains
Like a chamois they were sure-footed in predawn mist
They were the sons of eagles and big cats
When they stood on peaks, their hero's knots were tongues of flame
Their sturdy frames were shaped by salt and mountain winds, right from birth
Freedom and dignity were embedded in their bones, they persisted
Stemming from an era that created epics, they were the last great generation
Children of nature and avatars of founding heroes
Aimé Césaire, you have not died, your receding shape is on the homeward road
You are not alone, for countless homeward travelers are with you
Souls of this world eternally yearning for native ground

September 5, 2011

诗歌的起源

诗歌本身没有起源，像一阵雾
它没有颜色，因为它比颜色更深
它是语言的失重，那儿影子的楼梯
并不通向笔直的拱顶
它是静悄悄的时钟，并不记录
生与死的区别，它永远站在
对立或统一的另一边，它不喜欢
在逻辑的家园里散步，因为
那里拒绝蜜蜂的嗡鸣，牧人的号角
诗歌是无意识的窗纸上，一缕羽毛般的烟
它不是鸟的身体的本身
而是灰暗的飞翔的记忆
它有起航的目标，但没有固定的港口
它是词语的另一种历险和坠落
最为美妙的是，就是到了行程的中途
它也无法描述，海湾到达处的那边
诗歌是星星和露珠，微风和曙光
在某个灵魂里反射的颤动与光辉
是永恒的消亡，持续的瞬间的可能性
是并非存在的存在
是虚无中闪现的涟漪
诗歌是灰烬里微暗的火，透光的穹顶
诗歌一直在寻找属于它的人，伴随生与死的轮回
诗歌是静默的开始，是对1加1等于2的否定
诗歌不承诺面具，它呈现的只是面具背后的叹息
诗歌是献给宇宙的3或者更多
是蟋蟀撕碎的秋天，是斑鸠的羽毛上撒落的
黄金的雨滴。是花朵和恋人的呓语
是我们所丧失、所遗忘的一切人类语言的空白
诗歌，睁大着眼睛，站在
广场的中心，注视着一个个行人
它永远在等待和选择，谁更合适？
据说，被它不幸或者万幸选中的那个家伙：
——就是诗人！

2011年9月7日

THE ORIGIN OF POETRY

Poetry itself has no origin, like a spell of fog
It has no color, because it underlies colors
It is language in free-fall, a staircase of shadow
Not climbing to the perfect lines of a dome
Its noiseless chronometer does not record
Distinctions of life and death; it stands against antipathy
But also against unification. It does not like to stroll
Where logic makes a home, for that is a place
That refuses the buzz of bees, the trumpet of a shepherd
Poetry is a twining wreath of smoke, shadowed on a paper window
Instead of the body of a bird
It is a gray memory of flight
It embarks for a goal, but has no definite harbor
It is an alternative exploit of discourse, a plummeting
How wonderfully odd that midway in its course
It cannot summon up scenes from its bay of arrival
Stars and dew, breeze and daybreak are refracted
With trembling brilliance through a soul, and that is poetry
It is an enduring disappearance, the possibility of an ongoing instant
It is existence that cannot exist
Like ripples that flash across nothingness
Poetry is the dimmed fire of embers, it is the transparent vault of sky
Poetry searches for those it owns, to follow its incarnations
Poetry is the beginning of silence, it denies that 1 + 1 = 2
Poetry does not approve of masks, lets us sense the sighs behind them
Poetry is an offering of three to the universe, or even more
It is the rending of autumn air by crickets, it is a golden droplet
Shaken from a turtledove's wing. It is flowers and murmurs of lovers
It is blankness from a human language that was lost or forgotten
Poetry stands wide-eyed in the middle of a plaza
Watching each and every passerby
Forever waiting and choosing, which one is suitable?
People say that the one who is chosen
That unlucky or oh-so-lucky fellow—is a poet!

September 7, 2011

我在这里等你

我曾经不知道你是谁?
但我却莫名地把你等待
等你在高原
在一个虚空的地带
宗喀巴也无法预测你到来的时间
就是求助占卜者
同样不能从火烧的羊骨上
发现你神秘的踪迹和影子
当你还没有到来的时候
你甚至远在遥遥的天边
可我却能分辨出你幽暗的气息
虽然我看不见你的脸
那黄金的面具,黑暗的鱼类
远方大海隐隐的雷声
以及黎明时草原吹来的风
其实我在这里等你
在这个星球的十字路口上
已经有好长的时间了
我等你,没有别的目的
仅仅是一个灵魂
对另一个灵魂的渴望!

2011年8月31日

I AM HERE WAITING FOR YOU

I knew not who you would be
Yet I found myself waiting for you
Waiting for you on a high plain
Waiting in a zone of emptiness
Not even Tsongkhapa could foretell your arrival*
Even a diviner would not be able
From a sheep's burned collarbone
To read any portent or inkling of you
Though you have not yet arrived
I can make out your elusive scent
As if far off at the edge of the sky
I cannot see your features
That golden mask, a school of fish in dark water
Thunder swallowed in a distant sea
Wind blowing at dawn over a grassland
In fact, I have been waiting here
At this crossroads of the world
For a long time
I await you for no other reason
It is simply the longing
Of one soul for another!

August 31, 2011

* Tsongkhapa (1357–1419) was the first patriarch of the Gelugpa (Yellow Hat) sect of Tibetan Buddhism.

吉勒布特的树

在原野上
是吉勒布特的树

树的影子
像一种碎片般的记忆
传递着
隐秘的词汇
没有回答
只有巫师的钥匙
像翅膀
穿越那神灵的
疆域

树枝伸着
划破空气的寂静
每一片叶子
都凝视着宇宙的
沉思和透明的鸟儿

当风暴来临的时候
马匹的眼睛
可有纯粹的色调?
那些灰色的头发和土墙
已经在白昼中消失

树弯曲着
在夏天最后一个夜晚
幻想的巢穴,飘向
这个地球更远的地方

这是黑暗的海洋
没有声音的倾听
在吉勒布特无边的原野
只有树的虚幻的轮廓
成为一束:唯一的光!

2011年9月4日

A TREE IN JJILE BUTE

There in the wilderness
Of Jjile Bute stands a tree

The shadow of the tree
Is like memory in fragments
Transmitting
A hidden vocabulary
There is no answer
Only a shaman's key
Like wings passing
Through the open range
Of spirit beings

Branches stretch
Cutting through quiet air
Each and every leaf
Envisions a meditating universe
And transparent birds

As a storm approaches
Could pure hues remain
In the eyes of a horse?
Colors of gray hair and earthen wall
Have vanished under the sun

The tree bends over
On summer's final evening
The den of fantasy drifts off
To an even more distant place on the globe

This is a sea of darkness
Listening without any sound
In the boundless wilderness of Jjile Bute
The tree's dreamlike silhouette
Appears in a beam: light like no other!

September 4, 2011

写给母亲

你怎能抗拒那岁月的波涛
一次次将堤岸——锤打!
怎能抗拒你的眼睛——我的琥珀玛瑙
失去了少女时的光泽
怎能阻止时间的杀手, 潜入光滑的肌肤
无法脱逃, 这魔法般的力量
修长的身材, 不等跨下新娘的马鞍
黑色的辫子, 犹如转瞬即逝的闪电
已变成稀疏的青丝
低垂下疲倦的头, 当下的事物已经模糊
童年的影子——陷入遥远的别离
青春的老屋——只从梦境里显现
闪光的银饰啊——彝人的女王
那百折裙的波浪让忌妒黯然失色
你目睹了人世间的悲欢和离合
向这一切告别——还没让你真的回望
所有的同代的姊妹啊——
都已先后长眠在火葬地的灵床
是的, 谁能安慰你——索取那逝去的日历!
是的, 谁能给予你——那无法给予的慰藉

FOR MOTHER

How can you fend off the surf of passing years?
On the breakwater of your lower back—you keep pounding!
How to defend your eyes—my vitrines and agates
That have lost their girlish sparkle
How to keep killer time from infiltrating your smooth skin?
There is nowhere to run from this demonic force
A slender figure hardly dismounted from a bridal saddle
Luster gone like lightning from raven locks now sparse
Weary head now lowered, things before you hazy
Shadows of childhood—gone off in the distance
Cottage of youthful years—appears in dreams
Gleam of silver pendants—regal matron of the Nuosu
Waves of pleated skirt cast envy into dark corners
Taken up with joys of union, pangs of parting
Streaming past your eyes—no chance to look back
The sisterly companions of your generation
Gone to their final rest at the cremation ground
Oh who can give—consolation that is no one's to give?
Who can comfort you—reclaim the pages of your calendar?

分裂的自我

我注定要置于分裂的状态
因为在我还没有选择的时候
在我的躯体里——诞生和死亡
就已经开始了殊死的肉搏
当我那黑色的意识
即将沉落的片刻
它的深渊却在升高
箭矢穿透的方向
既不朝向天堂!
更不面向地狱!
我的一部分脸颊呈现太阳的颜色
苦荞麦的渴望——
在那里自由地疯长
而我的另一部分脸颊
却被黑暗吞噬
消失在陌生城市的高楼之中
我的左耳能听见
一千年前送魂的声音
因为事实证明——
它能承受时间的暴力
它能用无形的双手
最快地握住——
那看不见的传统和血脉
它能把遗忘的词根
从那冰冷的灰尽中复活
然而,我的右耳却什么也听不见
是钢铁的声音已经将它杀死!
我的两只眼睛
一只充满泪水的时候
另一只干渴如同沙漠
那是我的眼睛
一只隐藏着永恒的——光明!
一只喷射出瞬间的——黑暗!
我的嘴唇是地球的两极
当我开口的时刻
世界只有死亡般的寂静
当我沉默寡言——
却有一千句谚语声如宏钟!
我曾拥有一种传承
而另一种方式却在我的背后
悄悄地让它消失

DIVIDED SELF

I am fated to be caught in a divided state
Before the choice was mine to make
Birth and death started grappling in my body
Making it their site of mortal conflict
As my recognition of noble blackness
Comes close to slipping away
Its abyss looms higher before me
Streaking in arrow-like flight
Not in the direction of heaven!
Not in the direction of hell!
One cheek is touched by sunlight
My longing for bitter buckwheat
Grows there like a hardy crop
But the cheek on the other side
Is swallowed in baneful darkness
Fading amid the towers of a strange city
My left ear can hear the soul-sending scripture
Voice chanting from a thousand years ago
Because facts have proven
It can endure the violence of time
Its impalpable hands can grip
The unseen tradition and bloodline
It can revive forgotten word roots
From the oblivion of cold ashes
Yet my right ear hears nothing
It has been killed by the sounds of iron!
And these two eyes of mine
Because of what they show me
When one is filled with tears
The other is parched like a desert
One is suffused with the light of eternity
One flickers with eruptions of darkness!
My lips are two poles of the earth
When my mouth opens to speak
The world falls into deathly stillness
When I hold my tongue
A thousand proverbs clang like bells!
I mastered a handed-down art
But could sense another form
Slipping away behind me

我永远在——差异和冲突中舞蹈
我是另一个吉狄马加
我是一个人
或者说——是另一只
不知名的——泪水汪汪的动物!

I dance a jig between contraries
I am another Jidi Majia
I am a man—or some other kind of animal
Seen through shimmering tears!